CLINTON'S PARTIAL LEGACY—WARS OF INTERDEPENDENCE

CLINTON'S PARTIAL LEGACY—WARS OF INTERDEPENDENCE

Nihilistic Nationalism and Imperious Imperialism

Robert R. Morman, PH. D.

Writers Club Press
San Jose · New York · Lincoln · Shanghai

Clinton's Partial Legacy—Wars of Interdependence Nihilistic Nationalism and Imperious Imperialism

Published by Writers Club Press
an imprint of iUniverse.com, Inc.

For information address:
iUniverse.com, Inc.
5220 S 16th, Ste. 200
Lincoln, NE 68512
www.iuniverse.com

ISBN: 0-595-12675-8

Printed in the United States of America

Dedication

This book is dedicated lovingly to my nieces and nephews that include Joseph, Robert (deceased) and Gerald Morman; Mary Ann Morman; Lois, Anthony and Nancy Presutti; Sandra, Sharon, Joanne and Richard Morman; Carol, Barbara, William, Jean and James Wallace; and Michelle and Joseph Moffa.

Epigraph
Uses its politica

Clinton's policies are reminiscent of an "old world" colonial nation
Uses its "'pol-econ'-high tech military" in "forced" negotiation
      Behavior that smacks egomaniacal,
      With odorous effects so tyrannical,
And a bully's disdain for each nation's past, culture, "gov" and organization

Why any nation would even want to surrender its sovereignty and nationalism
To "non-elected," one world ideologues and their unreal, utopian idealism
      Is incomprehensible, stupid, insane,
      A quixotic dream best perceived as a bane,
When their base motives are "political-social power and control through mercantilism"

Contents

Preface

This book is only a small portion of the sordid tale that describes Clinton's role in the relentless pursuit of a New World Order to the ultimate subjugation and detriment of the United States. A series of preliminary yet relatively safe military incursions were designed to pursue relentlessly the ideological one world objective of "subjugating" every nation on planet earth into slave-like status. The plan intends to "neutralize each nation's sovereignty to name only" and relinquish nationalist sovereign control to the dictates of "appointed, not elected" one world ideologues and bureaucrats who espouse similar aspirations to those of "sell out America" Clinton.

In order to justify U. S. military intervention into the internal affairs of sovereign nations, Clinton's White House propaganda machine left few possibilities to the imagination. Over the course of time, it rationalized that "rebuilding a nation, restoring a left wing politician to the 'seat of power,' righting human rights, maintaining international peace, involving blatantly a 'fictitious' vital national security interest, averting human disaster and demonstrating superpower status and global responsibility were sufficient justifications."

Additional propagandist "justifications" encompassed morality, humanitarianism, killing field avoidance, concentration camp deterrence, ethnic cleansing, combating terrorism, Balkan area stability and "acting now is less risky and costly than further delay." Further utopian justifications included "undefined geopolitical interests, credibility of the U. S., prevention of massacres, containment of war, affect on foreign policy, quest for ill defined long term interests, support of NATO's opposition to

aggression—'except—hypocritically' its own, fighting for future generations, phony "right thing to do—like eating oatmeal," trumped up requests
for assistance, installing freedom and democracy and the White House's
ancient, ever popular tear-jerker and raison d'être—"it's for the children.'"

Criticisms of any argument against foreign entanglement with even a
tinge of "isolationism, independence, nationalism, patriotism, U. S.
Constitution, Bill of Rights, allegiance to the U. S., the American Flag
and oath of office" were quickly and devastatingly denigrated with the
assistance of a willing media.

Isolationism was and is "falsely" depicted as a dirty word. Nothing
could be farther from the truth. The beneficial-to-the-United States defi-
nition refers to "not" ceding our sovereignty to arrogant "non-elected"
internationalists and international bureaucrats, warnings by our founding
fathers against foreign entanglements and totally ignoring the fact that
this greatest nation on earth was established after an arduous, bloody
"Revolutionary War was fought for *independence*" against England's tyrannical imperialism (nee colonialism). To sacrifice Revolutionary War won
independence for global-meddling wars of interdependence was Clinton's
cowardly, uncouth concession of U. S. sovereignty without "America
First" justification. His acts were and continue to be "UNAmerican."

That the United States is the world's leading "red ink" commercial
trader with deficits rising, harbor for coolie labor imports, champion of
world-wide tourism, leader in student exchange education, refuge for
refugees from countless nations, select haven of choice by "legal and illegal"
immigrants, annual supplier of volunteer Peace Corps workers worldwide,
disseminator of religious-medical missionaries, supreme humanitarian
nurturer in time of catastrophe anywhere in the world —but rarely vice
versa and largest international dole distributor to countless welfare nation-
recipients attests to our global involvement. The "isolation" argument
equates to Clinton's White House propagandist hogwash typical and
reflective of its "spin doctoring" policies.

To answer the "isolationist bashers," ask yourself a few pertinent questions. Which country in the world does more "for other nations"— without recompense or even an expression of gratitude than the United States? "How many of the international nation welfare recipients vote with the U. S. on international issues in the United Nations?" "How many of the international welfare recipient nations contribute even "token or nil" military forces to international peacekeeping operations?" "How many international welfare recipient nations contribute directly to international disasters?" "How many "substantial" benefits to the United States can you list as a result of meddling in the internal affairs of sovereign nations?" (What—cat got your pen?) More pertinent questions could easily be posed if pressed.

Chapter 1 describes chronologically the invasion of Somalia, initiated by former President Bush under the guise of rendering humanitarian assistance to a non-existent government loosely "governed" by various factions led by rambunctious rebel leaders. Turkish General Bir who had difficulty communicating with U. S. military forces commanded United Nations' forces. The war ended shortly after the world witnessed the dragging of a dead U. S. serviceman's body through city streets and U. S. troops ignominiously withdrew.

In the process of nation meddling, the policy of foolish "nation building" never really got started and the chief rebel leader, Aidid, remained scot-free. Incidentally, Somalia didn't "invite" a peaceful invasion of its sovereign territory or did the U. S. have a "commercial or national security interest" there.

Next discussed is the "chaotic" situation that existed in Haiti and Clinton's primary rationale for invading that destitute country. The "manifest" reason given was to "restore leftist Aristides to power in a democracy that never was." The more convincing "latent" reason, it is believed, was actually a "practice run" for one-world proponents to acclimate the American populace to the modus operandi of passively "accepting meddling in the internal civil affairs of a relatively weak and powerless sovereign nation."

Fortunately, the invasion of Haiti turned out to be a "bloodless, peaceful invasion" due to the sterling efforts of ex President Carter, retired General Powell and former Senator Nunn. Their successful negotiations spared Clinton, Christopher, Lake and Talbot from further adverse diplomatic embarrassment. Incidentally, the U. S. "never had any national security interest in Haiti." And, Haiti is still in chaos!

The situation in Bosnia led Clinton to order 20,000 troops for "peacekeeping" deployment without the approval of Congress, Veterans of Foreign Wars and the general public. He continually lied to the American people regarding their "tour of duty," left "open" the exit date of American forces and vowed to "veto any bill that contained a specific withdrawal date." A contingency force of 8,000 troops still remains in Bosnia on "indefinite deployment." Incidentally, the U. S. had "no national security interest in Bosnia."

The air strikes on suspected terrorist outposts in Afghanistan and Sudan turned out as two more examples of arrogant, prima donna Clinton's abject failures. The main terrorist sought, Osama bin Laden, was never killed in Afghanistan and the alleged chemical weapons factory in Sudan was actually a pharmaceutical company producing pharmaceuticals. The attacks coincided with the time of Clinton's court-ordered testimony given in the Paula Jones case and his televised revelation that "he did not have sexual relations with that women (Monica Lewinsky)." Incidentally, the U. S. had "only specious, marginal terrorist national interests in Afghanistan and Sudan."

Iraq and its "continuing threat to the Near East" has been a thorn in the side of American foreign policy ever since the "Desert Storm" victory that left Iraq intact with Saddam Hussein still in power, the result of former President Bush's inept, bumbling diplomacy. The issue of "locating and destroying" the production and storage of chemical, biological and nuclear weapons continues with fruitless findings.

The four days of conventional bomb and cruise missile strikes ordered by Clinton were criticized by Republicans. They charged the president with "orchestrating a crisis" on the eve of impeachment proceedings in an attempt to soften "political peril." Again, no mention was made of vital "national security interests" at the time.

Chapter 2 describes the sorry mess that still remains after Clinton ordered devastating air strikes on Kosovo in order to halt "ethnic cleansing" of Albanians by Serbians. Any previous Albanian terrorist insurrection actions were totally ignored by the U. S. Clinton and his inept political strategists erroneously believed the war would be over quickly after a few days of devastating air strikes inflicted preponderantly by the only super-power, the United States.

Clinton ordered the air strikes without sanction by the United Nations' Security Council because he knew full well that China and Russia would veto the vote. The quick air strike strategy failed, however, and the political strategists retreated to their planning bunker in the White House War Room. Hence, the decision was made to continue the war, escalate a vast propaganda campaign to convince the American public that Clinton's War was justified. The public, however, never really bought Clinton's nation-meddling propaganda.

Chapter 3 describes the stark realization that Clinton's "instant solution" war strategy was a dismal failure. After the first week of intense bombing, Milosevic was still in power, ethnic cleansing escalated, exodus of refugees from Kosovo increased, Milosevic's peace proposal was rejected and "widening of the war" became the "new" strategy.

In addition, a preliminary plan for re-locating displaced refugees was developed and quickly revised to accommodate Muslims and other interested parties, three American soldiers were captured by Serbia and Albania's imperialistic dreams in the Balkans are described.

The next chapter, 4, describes the intensification of the war, Clinton's plan to accept refugees and reactions, NATO's 50th anniversary celebration in Washington not Brussels; alas, "without victory's plum in Serbia."

Also discussed are NATO's new policy of "intervention for any reason extended beyond its 19 nation confines, lack of House support for ground troops and air strikes, release of three POWs, rejection of new peace feelers to end the war and arrival of the first group of refugees in America.

Chapter 5 discusses the errant bombing of the Chinese Embassy and repercussions, NIMA's out-of-date mapping errors and faulty intelligence and release of the POWs to Jesse Jackson that caused severe "diplomatic bragging distress" in the White House. Peace talks in the air, Los Angeles fetes the POWs, merciless resumption of air strikes, indictment of Milosevic and other war criminals, Milosevic's latest peace pact conditions and continuance of air strikes are also described.

Milsoveic's acceptance of the peace plan, signing of the peace plan, details of the "pull out" of Serb forces from Kosovo, provisions of the peace plan and confirmation of troop withdrawal are related in Chapter 6. Also discussed are Russian troops and the Pristina Airport affair, KLA's revengeful reactions to Serb troop withdrawal and costs and criticisms of Clinton's War for "interdependence."

Chapter 7 gives accounts of Serbian troop withdrawal, KFOR occupation and the aftermath that resulted in "reverse ethnic cleansing" of Serbs and Gypsies by Albanians. Other details are furnished concerning the slaughter of Serbs at Gracko, replacing General Clark with General Ralston as NATO commander, continuing Serbian-Albanian acrimony and four months after NATO's incursion into Kosovo.

Subsequent events are discussed including the exodus of 120,000 Serbs from Kosovo leaving only 80,000 behind as residents and the proposed creation of a "Continental Army" by European nations "independent of NATO and U. S. control." Politically, leaders in the U. S. and NATO oppose such a creation because their exclusive control of Europe's military and their one world objective would be in jeopardy.

Additionally described is the issue of "peaceful coexistence" between Albanian Muslims and Serbian Orthodox Christians considered largely "mythical" by General Reinhardt and others. Pockets of armed conflicts still exist, armed engagements are continuing and the situation remains flammable.

The succeeding chapter, 8, relates essentials concerning Clinton's imperialism in the Middle East including a bit of background of the volatile situation, status of a Palestinian state and author's perception of a separate Palestine. It would not be surprising in the not too distant future to witness similar tactics for "autonomy and independence" employed in Kosovo used by Palestinians in Israel.

Chapter 9 is a synopsis of events regarding East Timor, province of Indonesia, and its rebellious desire for "autonomy and independence." Specifics concerning background of the problem, International Military and Education Training or IMET, international pressure exerted to invite UN meddling, IFOR's entry into East Timor, criticisms of Clinton's action in East Timor and aftermath are discussed. It marked the first occasion in which the U. S.—NATO military union extended its nation meddling tentacles to the Far East.

Other provinces like Aceh, Indonesia and Chechnya, Russia, possible ripe sites for U. S.—NATO meddling in the internal affairs of sovereign nations, are described in Chapter 10. Indonesia does not wish for their "forcefully imposed peaceful assistance" in Aceh. Besides, Indonesia knows Aceh is "resource rich" and is not about to abandon its wealth.

Also discussed are Russia's intentions to preserve its territorial integrity, stave off Albright's threats of "diplomatic isolation" and delay IMF and Export—Import Bank loans. They were considered as hollow threats and would not cow Russia into submission.

Also described is the stupidity of even considering a direct confrontation with "friendly foe" Russia at this time as mostly "bluff and bluster" and "wisely out of the question." It is by means a small, backward or non-industrialized nation but has formidable armed forces that include land, air, naval and a foreboding nuclear capability. (Recall Napoleon's disastrous debacle and Hitler's insane invasion of Russia.)

Chapter 11 relates the "nationalist" uprising in Austria that defies U. S.—NATO meddling and may serve to spark further resurgence of nationalism in other European nations. Particulars concerning Haider's Freedom Party and Schuessel's People's Party uniting into a duly elected coalition government, fitful UN threats of diplomatic isolation and freezing contracts, Haider's resignation from the Freedom Party and other pertinent matters are discussed.

Other European foci of "patriotic nationalist resurgence" are discussed in Chapter 12. Countries like Belgium, Italy, France, Spain, Germany, Turkey and the African Congo have politically active "nationalist parties led by extremist rebels" who place loyalties with their countries first. In common, they all detest borderless immigration with its attendant societal ills and vehemently oppose enslaved subjugation to "mini, one-world U. S.—NATO meddling" in the internal affairs of sovereign nations along with other deleterious issues.

The last chapter, 13, is a closing statement and account of Clinton's Wars of "interdependence and foreign meddling," a shameful partial legacy for this president. His "America Second" policy bodes ill for the future "independence, sovereignty and freedom from foreign entanglements" of the United States. That is, unless the U. S. Congress and the citizenry awake from their submissive slumber.

Chapter 1

"Practice Invasions" for Clinton's U. S., UN—NATO Meddling In the Internal Affairs of Sovereign Nations

Prior to Clinton's military meddling in the internal affairs of Somalia, Haiti, Bosnia, Afghanistan, Sudan, Iraq, Kosovo, Israel and East Timor, the essentially defenseless countries of "mighty" Grenada and "puissant" Panama had been invaded by powerful imperialistic U. S. military forces. The U. S. military invasions into Grenada and Panama occurred after former President Bush—zealous, ardent exponent of the One World Order issued the orders.

The genesis of Clinton's authority to meddle in the internal affairs of other nations was formally executed when he signed the "Policy of Reforming Multilateral Peace Operations" as a Presidential Decision Directive 13 (PDD) on May 31, 1994 according to Schlafly. PDD 13 delegated operational control of U. S. forces to a foreigner who reported to the UN Security Council. It transferred surreptitiously war powers from the U. S. Congress to a multilateral organization under the aegis of the United Nations.

It was designed to subordinate the U. S. military to a multinational authority. The "meddling in the internal affairs of sovereign nations" directive "allowed" the U. S. to combat "current threats to peace" that encompassed "territorial disputes, armed ethnic conflicts, civil wars and the collapse of governmental authority." "Peacekeeping" was broadened to allow the American military to "promote democracy, regional security and economic growth worldwide."

The ever-duplicitous "Slick One" informed the media that "the U. S. would never relinquish command authority over U. S. forces, but on a case-by-case basis, would "consider placing them under operational control of a 'competent' UN commander for specific UN operations authorized by the United Nations Security Council."

Schlafly commented that Presidential Decision Directive 13 was the "first unconstitutional transfer of power" in the history of the nation. It was a "secret sell-out directive" with important "need to know" details kept hidden from the American people. Cowardly, clever Clinton released only a summary of PDD 13 to the media and kept secret many other details.

In June 1994, President Clinton told our allies that "we must band together to stop the 'disease of militant nationalism' in Bosnia and elsewhere." And, "UN control of U. S. military forces was the rule in all three countries," presumably meaning Iraq, Somalia with its "competent commander" and Bosnia.

Senator Lugar asserted there was no significant congressional support for Clinton's policies concerning Somalia, Bosnia or Haiti wrote Lewis, September 15, 1993.

Somalia

U. S. involvement in Somalia was initially ex President Bush's decision, i. e., to meddle into the internal affairs of a sovereign nation under the guise of "humanitarianism." At the time, Somalia had not requested assistance, didn't have a stable government and most Americans had never even heard of the country or knew of its location. At no time did the U. S. ever have either a "commercial or national security interest in Somalia."

Citizen Spangler, August 1993, believed Somalia represented a break-through for New World Order promoters under the guise of "human decency and without invitation."

Buchanan, September 1993, wrote that Secretary of Defense Aspin dispatched 400 Rangers including Delta Force commandos to remain in Somalia until a credible police force could be installed. Aspin declared that "it was not enough to deliver food." It was glaringly obvious that U. S. vital interests never existed in Somalia.

Buchanan suggested that PDD 13, the directive that authorized U. S. intelligence and U. S. troop control transferred to the UN, be rescinded and that U. S. forces not be used for peacekeeping purposes. He astutely perceived the latter purpose would constitute an "endless trap."

The "UN" force in Somalia eventually numbered 28,000 troops led by Turkish General Bir whose forces were incompetent in communicating with U. S. troops without American leadership.

The eventual outcome of meddling in Somalia ended in failure to capture the rebel leader, Aidid, a tortuous dragging of a U. S. soldier through its streets, an ignominious withdrawal of U. S. armed forces and a face-saving token military presence thereafter.

Haiti

Draft dodger Clinton ordered the invasion of the tiny defenseless island of Haiti while an eleventh hour agreement for "peace" was being negoti-ated. Political negotiations focused on a plan to return Aristide, alleged communist, to "head a democratic government that never was," grant amnesty to the military junta, protect the Haitian Army from retribution, pay three thousand dollars each to convert former Haitian Army soldiers into police officers and pay a disarming bounty for all guns turned in by its citizens.

Clinton's "multinational peaceful invasion force" was 100 percent American and consisted of 20 ships, 6,000 elite troops, 9,000 soldiers held in reserve plus all military equipment and aircraft. Even the farcical "token" military contributions from member nations of the UN were "conspicuously absent" from Clinton's imperialistic "crisis" operation.

The proposed "multinational occupational force or farce" would retrain the Haitian Army, train a new civilian police force, maintain order and secure the operation for Aristede's safe return. After the invasion "secured" Haiti, a "barely token" multinational occupational force comprised of 1,000 members from 25 other wholeheartedly concerned UN member nations would absurdly "take over!"

Fortunately, successful diplomatic efforts negotiated by cooler heads, Jimmy Carter, Colin Powell and Sam Nunn, averted Clinton's crisis ordered "hostile Haitian invasion" by urging the military junta to step down. The military junta agreed to leave office by October 15, 1994. By dint of the successful efforts of the "effective diplomatic trio without port-folio," American casualties were completely averted.

The agreement saved Clinton's White House and the U. S. State Department from the embarrassment of a hostile invasion, possible loss of lives, injuries and negative public reaction—since czarist-like Clinton acted virtually "alone." It also spared the collective, unsuccessful alleged diplomatic prowess and rear ends of White House policy echoes Christopher, Lake and Talbot from further public chagrin and castigation.

In making the decision to invade Haiti, determined, dedicated "one world" Clinton, purposely ignored opposition from the Organization of American States, other world nations, world public opinion, the American public and the U. S. Congress. In effect, the draft dodger thumbed his nose at everyone.

An Associated Press news item revealed that Clinton issued an open-ended order that hundreds of troops would remain in Haiti to prevent the possibility of chaos. The current order was scheduled to expire on December 31, 1999.

In his customary duplicitous fashion, Clinton denied making an "indefinite commitment" but did make a "definite commitment" to being involved in an "appropriate" way. Clinton's order insured that U. S. troops would be the "last to leave" just as they were the "first to enter" Haiti.

Later, Canadian and Pakistani "peacekeepers" reported the mission would be one of "support not combat." The "social support" role for 300—500 U. S. troops would be involved by working in civil affairs, building roads, digging wells, repairing schools and providing medical assistance.

Senator Helms called the order "foolhardy and unconscionable" for U. S. troops to remain after the usual number of token UN peacekeepers departed. He questioned Albright to justify how a small training contingent of U. S. troops could achieve more than a $2 billion "unilateral" U. S. troop invasion and presence in Haiti for the past three years.

A few congressional critics feared Haitian violence could erupt in putting the wee U. S. force at risk. The Pentagon retorted that 150 U. S. Military Police "provided security" for the military (or social worker if you prefer) force.

Fineman reported that Haiti and Democracy had sunk into disorder since President Preval postponed elections indefinitely. Aristide had been replaced because of a one-term limit imposed by Haiti's Constitution.

It appeared the rule of law had broken down and democracy was imperiled. The judiciary was deemed dysfunctional. The State Department reported extra judicial killings by the police. Lawlessness seemed to prevail.

Elections were postponed for reasons of lack of registration cards, too few registration offices and long lines of voter registrants. The UN's Organization of American States said that no one knew how many Haitians there are.

As the writer mused in "Clinton's Planned Betrayal of America 'UNAmericanization," the invasion of Haiti was perhaps the prelude to sending troops to Bosnia. Clinton would capitalize on congressional inertia, minimal public agitation, man-in-the-street apathy and interventionist confidence.

Bosnia

Columnists named Safire, McCartney, Buchanan and Slevin warned early on that sending troops to Bosnia was foolish because no U. S. interests were at stake. The U. S. Congress, Veterans of Foreign Wars and the general public were opposed to sending troops as well. Safire, August 31, 1993, reported that sending troops to Bosnia would be a monumental mistake. He emphasized the American people had no desire to be involved in Bosnia.

Columnist McCartney, October 15,1993, penned that Clinton offered to supply 20 thousand troops in a peacekeeping mission—"if there ever was one!" Buchanan, October 15, 1993, advised Clinton to forget about the "enlargement of democracy everywhere as U. S. policy and using U. S. troop for peacekeeping." Such policies were simply an endless egregious trap.

Sleven didn't believe U. S. involvement in Bosnia would affect a permanent solution because "excessive nationalism" still reigned in the hearts of all ethnic groups.

Nevertheless, crafty Clinton "took it upon himself" to order 20,000 U. S. troops to Bosnia in November 1995. After troop deployment, Clinton embarked on a national whitewash campaign to "convince" Americans that the tactic was essential for "peace, world leadership, guilty conscience, morality, basic principles, boy scout training, impressing extra-curricular girlfriends, feelings of inferiority, show of bravado" and other irrelevant justifications. (The author asked, "Why, was it ever necessary to 'sell' the American people on involvement in Bosnia without any real national security interest?")

To no one's surprise, Clinton's action was supported by job-beholding, political appointees and echoes of his policies including Christopher, Albright, McMurry, Perry, Talbot and others.

One soldier, courageous Army Specialist Michael New, refused to wear the "UN blue or serve under a foreign command." He had taken a soldier's oath to defend the U. S. Constitution, not the United Nations. In retaliation, the U. S. Army proceeded promptly to label New as "a potential cancer" and dishonorably discharged him. The Army tried to justify its action in order to "prevent other activist, loyal, dedicated, patriotic, red-blooded American soldiers'" from displaying their "primary allegiance to the American Flag" or violating their solemn oath "to defend the U. S. Constitution" unlike the devious draft-dodging commander-in-chief residing in the White House!

At the time, Defense Secretary Perry commented that the U. S. military would assume "police, people movement, grave excavation, search for war criminals, social welfare and related duties" to fulfill UN objectives in the "second, new socialistic world order." Indeed, the U. S. military proceeded to assume its new role, that of "international social worker!"

In 1995, Clinton said 20 thousand troops would be deployed for a year. One year later (1996), 8,000 troops were still in Bosnia. "Candid" Clinton then told America the troops would be out by June 1998. Later, when troop presence in Bosnia was "up for discussion," candor-less Clinton promised to "veto any bill that contained a specific withdrawal date."

Clinton decided to keep U. S. peacekeeper troops in Bosnia beyond June 1998 wrote Bennet. In December 1997, 8,000 U. S. troops were still stationed in Bosnia as part of NATO's 30,000 plus forces. How many U. S. troops would remain after June 1998 was not mentioned in the column.

Originally Clinton stated U. S. troops would only stay one year—until the end of 1996, then extended this assignment to June 1998.

Bennet described fibber Clinton's escape from a Bosnian "deadline"
    Admitted he'd been wrong; would not a definite date certain "assign"
    Our "social worker" troops must rebuild
    Schools, roads and a new "econ-pol" field,
While the "enforced cease fire" deterred our exit to "somewhere down the line".

Ross described Clinton's "week-end" trip to Bosnia in December 1997 that "celebrated" with American troops and emphasized the need for a continued presence to forestall any outbreak of hostility. Former Senator Robert and Libby Dole, Senator Stevens, Representative Kasich and nine other unnamed congressional representatives accompanied Clinton.

> Clinton, Hillary and Chelsea arrived in Bosnia to spread Christmas cheer
> Perhaps felt "obligated," because he "is" the sole reason the troops are here
> Hoped a "homey" touch might be added with their presence,
> To soften orders to "keep them there" was the essence,
> On an "indefinite tour of duty" that he'd already made rather clear

Secretary of Defense Cohen also played the duplicitous Clinton word game by noting the difference between an "indefinite" and "infinite" tour of duty. His statement was an oxymoron since life on earth itself is fast, fleeting and finite, not infinite, including any American soldier's tour of duty.

Bennet discussed Clinton's Christmas visit to Bosnia where he urged the troops to "do their part" in overcoming ethnic hatred, living in harmony and indicting war criminals. Clinton's orders to U. S. troops deployed in Bosnia would extend beyond June 1998, but "thankfully—not forever."

The "Clinton family trip" to Bosnia smacked of obvious intent to capitalize on positive PR, Chelsea's presence for favorable photo opportunities and brief family vacation.

Afghanistan and Sudan

Polay, managing editor of the Cape Cod Journal, described Clinton-ordered "crisis" bombing raids by American forces on suspected terrorist outposts located in Afghanistan and Sudan on August 19, 1998. The Commander-in-Chief claimed the actions were "necessary" because of recent terrorist bombings in Kenya and Tanzania. Clinton asserted that U. S. intelligence had "compelling information" that terrorists were planning further attacks and attempting to acquire chemical weapons.

After issuing the order, while on vacation at Martha's Vineyard, "crisis" Clinton flew back of Washington to confer with his National Security Council staff. Hillary and Chelsea, however, remained at the vacation resort.

Even before Clinton returned to Washington, his order to launch strikes against suspected terrorist sites in Afghanistan and Sudan were deemed "suspicious" by several U. S. Senators and the minister of Sudan according to Hogenson.

Senator McCain was "disappointed" Clinton hadn't consulted with congressional leaders before ordering the air strikes.

Senator Coats commented, "Timing of the attacks was extraordinary and uncharacteristic of anything Clinton had done during his presidential tenure and certainly raised legitimate questions."

Perhaps more damning was the revelation by the minister of Sudan that "the target was not a chemical weapons plant but a factory for making pharmaceuticals!"

The timing of the attacks was immediately preceded by two "coincidental events." Ninety-six hours before the order to launch was given, Clinton was ordered to give testimony before a federal grand jury concerning possible commission of perjury or obstruction of justice in the Paula Jones sexual harassment case. On the following Monday, August 18, 1998, Clinton appeared on national television to "admit" he had an "inappropriate relationship with that woman (Monica Lewinsky). During testimony Clinton gave to prosecutors earlier in the week, Clinton refused to answer certain questions.

A report by Md. Sadiq related that Clinton's air strikes ordered against suspected "terrorist related facilities" in Afghanistan and Sudan were in retaliation for recent bombings in Nairobi and Dar-es-Salam. Seven suspected terrorist sites were attacked in Afghanistan and a suspected chemical weapons facility in Sudan.

The article added that Clinton claimed to have "convincing evidence" that terrorists were involved in U. S. Embassy bombings where 11 innocent Americans had been killed in Nairobi and Dar-es-Salam. Clinton added the usual "jerry-built" justification for the air attacks—"terrorists threatened our national security."

Anderson, president of Probe Ministries International, commented on the bombing of the chemical plant in Sudan. He conducted a thorough analysis of the situation in Sudan and provided the following findings.

The chemical plant was not heavily guarded according to Carnaffin, a British Engineer who previously worked at the plant and recalled employees were free to walk everywhere. In addition, corporate records revealed that a Saudi Arabian banker owned it.

Further, the plant produced malaria tablets for children and drugs for livestock, pill bottles were found in the debris, soil samples showed no evidence of VX nerve gas and glass-lined reactors were not found thereby providing mute evidence that it was not a chemical weapons factory. Lastly, no one died of VX nerve gas poisoning and firefighters were not photographed fighting flames.

In sum, Anderson concluded there was no hard evidence that the facility was a chemical weapons plant. Alleged claims that it was a "strategic target" remained under suspicious.

Columnist Reese opined that Clinton had committed an "act of war" against Afghanistan and Sudan with its ensuing air strikes based on "whim." Reese believed that the bombing of four targets in Afghanistan and a chemical factory in Khartoum, Sudan were connected to Clinton's sex life and his televised assertion, "I did not have sexual relations with that woman."

The bombings demonstrated that "the U. S. government had no respect for international law, intensified hatred against the U. S., increased terrorist attacks and alienated the entire Muslim world."

The bombings blew up latrines, tents, canvas scraps, oil barrels and rifle targets at four suspected terrorist sites in Afghanistan. Reese called it a "brilliant" military strike costing millions of dollars that was ordered by an administration "famous for lying."

Reese wagered that the bombing in Khartoum had nothing to do with chemical weapon production while unknown numbers of innocent civilians were likely killed.

He observed that similar "reprisal raids" had been a tactic of Israel for 50 years, failed miserably to deter terrorist attacks, appealed to machismo and ego and proved counterproductive.

Reese lamented the fact that decision-makers failed to see the "consequences of their acts." He thought that committing "reprisal attacks on a whim" alienated the entire Muslim world. With regard to Afghanistan and Sudan, neither nation had the power to declare war on the U. S., the only reigning superpower; therefore, they should gain worldwide sympathy.

Reese concluded his article by writing that thanks to a corrupt political system, the U. S. was being destroyed including the opportunity for a real peace.

The author wondered if the alienation of the entire Muslim world had a political connection to Clinton's decision to invade Kosovo under the guise of "stopping ethnic cleansing." Did a nexus exist to "right the wrongs" of Afghanistan and Sudan, assuage the animosity of Muslims and motivate Clinton to subsequently order air strikes on Serbian Christians in Kosovo and side with Albanian Muslims?"

Iraq

Clinton ordered air strikes against Iraq on December 16, 1998 after a year of threatening to attack because it refused to allow entry to UN arms inspectors and the destruction of its chemical, biological and nuclear weapons described Parker and Towle. Clinton said, "We had to act and act now." At the same time, the Pentagon planned to deploy 40,000 troops in the Persian Gulf.

Clever, conniving Clinton had "put off" the attack a month ago when Hussein promised to comply with UN arms inspectors. One month ago, however, the timing was apparently not considered propitious for a

"Clinton concocted crisis." Since Hussein reneged on his promise, "air strike bombardier" Clinton was "prepared to act without delay, diplomacy or warning." His Joint Chief of Staff Shelton, one ally—Britain and national security advisers concurred with his decision.

"Operation Desert Fox" began at 9:00 a. m., Eastern Standard Time, with 50 Navy strike fighters—F-14 Tomcats and FA-18 Hornets from the aircraft carrier U. S. S. Enterprise ordered into combat. Shortly thereafter, U. S. warships fired more than 200 Tomahawk cruise missiles into southern Iraq.

A primary Iraqi bombing target was its air defense system. The U. S. Navy's radar-seeking HARM missiles were designed to render them inoperable in preparation for heavy bombing by U. S. A. F. B-52s and attacks by British Tornado fighters. Other specific targets were military sites and military units. The B-52s and Tornadoes were scheduled to attack later at night. Daylight lulls would allow reconnaissance with photographs to evaluate the effectiveness of the air strikes.

"Independent" Secretary of Defense Cohen, White House "military meddling" policy echo, was sure Clinton's decision to bomb was "absolutely right" and, at the same time, was sensitive to the upcoming Muslim holiday—Ramadan. Satellite and aircraft reconnaissance had shown the Iraqi were only "partially prepared" for an attack but offered no further rationale for timing of the attack. Cohen insisted the air attacks were not a distraction; rather, it was in the American public's best interest!

Senator Chaffee and others supported the air strikes. Senator Lott, however, complained the air strikes were "coincidentally timed" to distract from pending impeachment hearings originally scheduled to begin today but temporarily postponed.

Broder and Crossette reported that Clinton planned the air strikes against Iraq two days before and relied on information obtained from chief weapons inspector Butler that Hussein was defying UN inspections. Butler told the president two full days earlier about the report's contents. Butler delivered the official report to the UN Security Council while Clinton was flying from a whirlwind trip to Jerusalem back to the White

House. While airborne, Clinton then issued a 71-hour countdown for the Pentagon to commence air strikes.

Butler's report contained little that was not available to American officials weeks earlier! The stage for military strikes had been tentatively set for "anytime" after December 1, 1998!

On the eve of impeachment, Republicans charged the president with "orchestrating a crisis" in order to put a crimp on mounting momentum toward impeachment. Butler rejected assertions from critics that he had timed his report due to political pressure to serve as a pretext for Clinton's air strikes. He said his report was based on facts gathered by UNSCOM experts and delivered on time as promised.

Clinton was careful not to offend Arab allies and Muslims because of impending Ramadan or his safety while he visited Israel.

The attack on Iraq was timed to occur on the "eve of impeachment"
After "consulting" with Albright et al. on "political sediment"
  "Careful" not to overlap with holy Ramadan,
  "Careless" about any damage to Iraq's Saddam,
As the "designer of diversion" orchestrated air strike bombardment.

Democrat Representative Gejdensen said incredibly there were "no other considerations than U. S. national security and the safety of service personnel" for Clinton's decision. He revealed that the "always available but anonymous" lawmaker feared Congress and the public would "misinterpret" Clinton's order as a distraction from his "political peril!" (Really! Preposterous! How could they possibly think that?)

After three days of air strikes on Iraq including 300 cruise missiles fired, only 18 of 88 targets were confirmed hits wrote Shenon. Military command centers, missile factories, television and radio transmitters and an oil refinery were among the selected targets. General Shelton reluctantly reported that all air strikes "did not go as planned."

Propaganda leaflets were also dropped on Iraq warning military units of further bombing raids from aircraft carriers at sea and air bases in the region if they mobilized. Saddam Hussein blasted Clinton and the U. S. for the air strikes and labeled his attackers "The agents of Satan."

General Shelton said more missiles were fired against Iraq in the first two days than were rained on Iraq in 1991. Each computer-guided bomb cost $1million. Cruise missiles were preferred to conventional "soft bombs" or "laser-guided missiles" since no pilots were involved. They were more accurate and induced fewer civilian casualties.

The U. S. sponsored Radio Free Iraq expanded its "anti-Baghdad government" programming and straight news to four hours.

> The "agents of Satan" were what Saddam labeled his attackers
> Said, "By God, we will not compromise with the Western bushwhackers;
>   We stand against the bad barbarians,
>   Who just 'pose' as humanitarians,"
> Cursed the foes who aggrieved our people like rapacious reactors.

Defense Secretary Cohen was "sensitive" to Ramadan, the month of religious reflection that began that day. It is the holiest time on the Islamic calendar. Nevertheless, air strikes would continue until U. S.—British officials determined that sufficient damage had been inflicted.

After four days, Clinton announced that the air strikes had been a success and our mission had been achieved wrote Wright and Daniszewski. More than 400 bomb and missile strikes destroyed significant military and command security structures.

Cohen declared that 14 air defense sites, nine chemical and biological weapon sites, 16 command-and-control sites and 16 security force installations were damaged.

He promised that the U. S. would maintain a strong military presence in the Persian Gulf ready to attack again if Hussein rebuilt his weapons of mass destruction or threatened Kurds or any neighboring states.

Surveillance of "no fly" zones would continue with any challenges to allied aircraft severely resisted.

Clinton intended to "degrade" Saddam's capacity to construct and deliver weapons of mass destruction that threaten the Persian Gulf region. He would continue economic sanctions that had already cost Iraq $120 billion and support political forces in Iraq opposed to Saddam's regime.

Clinton also tried to assure Iraq's neighbors that he acted because of "internal threats to Iraq's people and the Arab world and possible external threats of biological, chemical and nuclear weapons." He would seek a "global consensus to help establish an Iraqi government worthy of its people."

> Saddam, in effect, told Clinton to "go pound desert sand"
> Would bar return of UN inspectors from Iraq's land
> > Said the price to get rid of UNSCOM
> > Was to suffer cruise missile and bomb,
> And what was destroyed would be rebuilt under his command.

Citizen Williams penned that clever, conniving Clinton used Saddam Hussein as the excuse to continue propelling the U. S. into a "world order" under the control of the U. S. but UN-dominated world government. Williams warned, "It was long past the time for the U. S. to maintain its sovereignty and quit the United Nations."

Myers wrote that the U. S. and Britain halted their attacks on Iraq as the holy month of Ramadan began in the world of Islam. Clinton called off the attacks "a few hours after the House voted to impeach him!"

> Saddam's Iraq, "battered—but unbowed," reacted with defiance
> Cooperation with UNSCOM not yet in servile compliance
> > The bombings ended with a "standoff,"
> > Arms "inspectors" received no "hand-off,"
> As Iraq emerged from bombings by the Clinton-Blair alliance.

Defense Secretary Cohen said the attacks set back Iraq's ballistic missile program "by at least a year." An anonymous military commander conceded to a setback but was reluctant to set a time certain.

Sometime in March 1999, the U. S. sent a spy to install the latest state-of-the-art electronic eavesdropping system in an effort to locate Saddam's secret weapon systems scribed Weiner. The spy entered Iraq "disguised" as a member of the UN weapons inspection team. With the device left in place at a select site when the UNSCOM was ejected, the U. S. was able to monitor cell phones, walkie-talkies and other communication devices that transmitted "intelligence."

U. S. spy practice for intelligence gathering purposes was not supposed to be allowed as part of UNSCOM's job description. The U. S. haughtily declared that it had the "blessings of Butler, U. S. chairman of UNSCOM." Apparently, the spy system didn't locate any sites of "mass weapons of destruction" since four days of cruise missile and conventional bombing failed miserably to pinpoint or obliterate them.

The column revealed that electronic eavesdropping started three years in 1995 and was later replaced by the U. S. spy. U. S. officials insisted that Butler and a few other unnamed UNSCOM members approved the covert program.

Despite assistance from defector, General Kamal, son-in-law of Saddam who returned to Iraq and was promptly shot his aides provided information on Iraq's security apparatus that had successfully secreted its biological, chemical and nuclear weapons systems since 1991. Iraq's "National Monitoring Directorate," the important target, had never been penetrated.

An Associated press news item reported that U. S. and British aircraft, after being targeted on a routine "no-fly" zone patrol, attacked artillery sites in northern and southern Iraq and killed 19 persons and wounded 10 others.

In addition, the U. S. European Command in Germany said that F-15s and F-16s bombed a missile site and missile support system near the city of Mosul.

Baghdad has repeatedly challenged enemy aircraft flying over its territory because it violated its sovereignty and international law.

The UN Security Council voted to re-start its search for Iraq's suspected weapons of mass destruction with the "bribe" of easing a nine-year economic sanction if they complied with arms inspection. It also lifted the cap of $5.2 billion in oil sales every six months to finance U. S. "supervised" purchases of humanitarian supplies.

Deep differences on the United Nations Security Council remained, however, since France, China and Russia—along with Malaysia could have vetoed the resolution but "abstained." Thus the vote failed to convey "unanimity."

China's Ambassador Huasan said the resolution, as passed, would not solve the Iraqi problem. France believed the "imprecise" resolution might maintain an indefinite delay regarding the sanctions and lead to new crises.

Saddam was encouraged by the "abstentions" to resist compliance in terms of expecting that France and Russia would be encouraged to contract for lucrative oil deals in Iraq.

The UN inspectors withdrew on December 16, 1998 when the U. S. and Britain launched air strikes coincident with the impeachment process. Since that time, Iraqi air defense have been almost daily subjected to bombing.

The newspaper, 11 Messaggero, felt that the U. S.—British air strikes against Iraq were a failure. Clinton couldn't explain the "legitimacy of his mission" or whose timing was suspiciously linked to the impeachment process. Britain's Blair militarily supported Clinton as "a sign of his historical, tactical and psychological submission."

The newspaper pointed out that Clinton and Europe failed to find a common political voice regarding Iraq.

Another newspaper, Frankfurter Allegemeine Zeitung, perceived U. S. policy toward Iraq as "helpless." The long-range policy view to oust Saddam was seen as disastrous and without an inkling of what to do next. The air strikes hurt Iraq's civilian population more than the military and increased Saddam's standing among the Arab nation.

Chapter 2

Kosovo and "Ethnic Cleaning"—Humanitarian Justification for Meddling

This chapter, along with chapters 3 through 7, describes the continued, relentless implementation of NATO's new "offensive" role and objective toward establishing a "mini One World Europe." The tragic tale is discussed chronologically under the sub headings of Prelude, Pact and Propaganda to Justify Air Bombardment of Kosovo; America's Bomb and Missile Destruction of Serbia Begins, Russia, Citizens, China et al. Protest the Air Strikes; Other Criticisms of Clinton's War, Responses to Criticisms of Clinton's War and Clinton's "Quick Air Strike Strategy" Failure. Other news releases are interspersed among the main headings.

Prelude, Pact, Propaganda and Precedent to Justify Air Bombardment of Kosovo

NATO's interference in the internal affair of a sovereign European nation, Serbia, served as one more "new world order" precedent and was revved up by propaganda issued from the Clinton administration and the media for U. S. public consumption. The province of Kosovo, Serbia was the site selected. Kosovo's Albanian militant population, "demanded independence by virtue of unrestrained immigrant inundation." In effect, the demands of Kosovo's guerrilla Albanians amounted to "insurrection and civil war" with a claim on land that didn't belong to them and the ultimate goal of building a Greater Albania.

Was this scenario not just another sordid, soiled scheme to sanction NATO's new deviously devised objective as a "U. S.—European global 'offensive' force (or farce if you prefer) to salvage the organization's" previous "defensive" objective toward containing Russian expansion and to implement a "mini European One World Order?"

An anonymous New York Times news blurb revealed that Milosevic ordered most units in Kosovo back to their barracks in a military "stand down" to avoid a possible air attack by NATO. The order brought a temporary end to burning and looting of villages.

Russia warned against the possible military intervention by NATO and dispatched its foreign and defense ministers to confer with Milosevic.

Roger Cohen's column, October 13, 1999, wrote that the U. S. and its allies in NATO "Okayed" the order for the U. S. to bomb Kosovo, a province of Serbia, in four days. U. S. Balkan envoy, Holbrooke, declared that Milosovic had agreed to withdrawal of forces, partial autonomy for Kosovo and the presence of a force of 2,000 UN "meddling monitors." The Serbian leader did not agree to cooperate with the Commission on International Crimes or CIC.

Clinton preferred to resolve the issue by "peaceful means," but would remain ready to take military action. Holbrooke agreed with globalist Clinton's threat of military force to "impose peace."

Hundley described the short-term settlement in that Milosevic agreed to a UN presence of 2,000 "civilian monitors to verify a cease fire" and "aerial verification by non combat NATO aircraft." He spoke of defending "Yugoslavia's dignity and national interests." Holbrooke's agreement did not provide for any international withdrawal of specific numbers of troops or heavy armaments.

Meanwhile, the Serbs continued their attacks against the Kosovo Liberation Army or KLA. Thus far, about 250,000 Kosovars had been left homeless and without shelter because of the belligerency.

Critic and historian, Proticia, observed that Milosevic was indispensable to negotiations because of "crisis spots" in Bosnia, Kosovo, eastern Slavonia and Macedonia since "peace depended on him."

Citizen Waters perceived the Muslims in Kosovo were "out breeding" the Christian Serbs

Demanding secession in massive cultural inundation that "provokes and perturbs"

U. S. thrusts into what we abhor,

A Serb-Albanian civil war,

And "led" by a Vietnam draft dodger who sent our forces into a war that disturbs.

Broder wrote that Clinton, in late February 1999, declared that the U. S. had "national and humanitarian" interests in resolving the conflict in order to maintain stability in the Balkans particularly in Kosovo that justified sending in ground forces as "peace troops." Clinton appointee, "let's bomb the hell out of them, peace-by-imposed force, mouthy, meddling, militant Madeline or C^4" concurred.

Albright remarked that Kosovar Albanians wouldn't sign the deal negotiated in Rambouillet unless the U. S. participated in its implementation. Serbian President Milosevic had not then agreed to the presence of international troops on Serbian soil.

A White House blurb noted that the House of Representatives voted for a "non-binding" resolution to back Clinton's proposal to send troops to Kosovo as per the Associated Press. Clinton was pleased, but Representative Tillie Fowler objected and the proposal "to send troops" was defeated.

Clinton said the "threshold had been missed" for the use of force in Serbia reported Broder. "We must act to prevent more massacres in the Balkans," said Clinton. He added, "Strikes could begin in days designed to reduce Serbia's military capability."

Senator Lott wanted Clinton to explain more details to the American people. Senator Nickles was not keen on the plan to attack, but Clinton ignored him and didn't want more people slaughtered. Apparently his rationale went beyond humanitarian concerns because Clinton informed the senators, "We must act. If we don't act, the war will spread. By not acting, they could affect our foreign policy and our 'vital interests!'" Of course, the latter "true" vital interests to justify foreign meddling and entanglement were fictional and never defined.

An Associated Press news item reported that Holbrooke's attempt at a diplomatic solution had failed. The envoy retreated to "reassess" continuance of negotiations.

Milosevic called the two rounds of peace talks "a fraud, because the U. S. and its European allies "dictated" the agreement's text before negotiations started—without consulting the state—meaning Yugoslavia whose interests were at stake." He wanted a "just and tenable solution." Milosevic said that the U. S. "should be ashamed for readying to use force against a small country protecting its territory against separatists and its people against terrorism."

America's Bomb and Missile Destruction of Serbia Begins

Broder reported that Clinton decided to order air strikes against Serbia on March 24, 1999 because "acting now is less risky and costly than further delays" in response to Milosevic's intransigence. As further "justification," "Globocop" Clinton intemperately said the strikes were necessary to "avert humanitarian disaster, serve America's questionable-at-best, undefined geopolitical interests, prevent killing fields and avoid concentration camps."

Clinton ordered air strikes against Serbia after much "contemplation"
"To act now not later" might resolve the Serb-Kosovo disputation
    "Our geopolitical interests at stake,
    Avoid needless suffering this conflict does make,
And Milosevic's license to kill might lead to "camps of concentration"

"Slick" used the "credibility" of U. S.—NATO as a rationalization
Our interests required a "quiet' Europe for increased commercialization
    Warned the fight couldn't be contained,
    That its flames would spread unrestrained,
Unless we forcefully intervened with meddling "global cop military action"

Clinton recalled that Milosevic only "cooperated" in Bosnia after his forces were attacked. There, Clinton sided with the "majority Muslims" not the "minority Serb Orthodox Christians." To no one's surprise, advisor Berger and Senator Lieberman supported Clinton's actions.

Milosevic objected to U. S. led NATO's intervention in a civil war that disregarded Serbia's national sovereignty. With a common bond of Slavic heritage, Yeltsin supported Milosevic.

Myers' column disclosed more details on NATO's "participation" in the first wave. It consisted of cruise missiles fired from six B-52s, four American warships, two U. S. submarines and a British submarine. Waves of F-117 fighter-jets and B-2 bombers from the U. S. and seven NATO nations followed without details furnished of the expected, respective usual "token contributions" from other NATO nations.

Most Serbian targets were air defenses and its command network that posed a threat to pilots. Defense Secretary Cohen revealed there was no loss of aircraft on the first day, but Serbia lost three MIGs. NATO's Secretary General Solana declared the air strikes were aimed at the government not the people.

No immediate estimates of casualties and damage were reported by Montgomery, Fleishman and Parker. The column repeated Clinton's reasons for the attack that included containment, humanitarianism, stability in the region and risks of acting outweighing risks of not acting. Clinton's goal was to "force Serbia to sign the 'imposed' peace deal with Kosovar Albanians and to support NATO's opposition to aggression" by hypocritically acting aggressively.

Historically, as in any alleged United Nations operation, the air strikes consisted mainly of American military might. The air battle groups and sea armada included eight B-52s, two B-2 stealth bombers and six U. S. warships that launched Tomahawk missiles, 1000 pound and 2000 pound bombs on military targets. NATO nations furnished the expected "token" forces, although the likely embarrassing details were not disclosed in the column.

The United Nations "token" contributions in men, materials, money, management and armament were akin to what other United Nations' members "magnanimously" contributed in Korea, Vietnam, Grenada, Panama, Somalia, Haiti, Sudan and Afghanistan but somewhat more in Bosnia.

An anonymously written news item revealed that "NATO gave 'mini one world Europe' pledges to protect Albania, Bulgaria, Macedonia, Slovenia and Romania and their concerns about threats to their security." At that time, Serbia had not attacked any of the above listed nations but did warn them not to support NATO's bombing or ethnic Albanian rebels.

Russia, Citizens, China et al. Protest the Air Strikes

A shocked Yeltsin protested U. S. led bombing of Serbia. He threatened undefined actions. Russia demanded an emergency UN session to lift the United Nations' arms embargo against Yugoslavia in order to supply arms. Russia recalled its envoy to NATO and suspended membership in "Partnership for Peace," a bipartisan union of nation friends and foes!

Russia had also failed in its attempt to influence the U. S. in halting air strikes on Iraq. It considered Serbia's orthodox Slavs as its historical ally. Prime Minister Primakov canceled a trip to Washington D. C. in mid flight and returned home. The purpose of his visit was to request "billions of dollars" in additional aid to bolster Russia's failing economy. In ominous fashion, Primakov did not think the strikes would "stabilize the situation; quite to the contrary,"

(It appeared that Russia's innocuous but fence-straddling bombast and bluster were reactions designed to render "face saving, loyal visible support" to Yugoslavia while not jeopardizing its dependence on financial relief from the U. S.)

Citizen Bozic called NATO's air strikes on Serbia as the first country to be attacked for protecting its historic motherland from terrorist guerrillas (KLA). He asked, "How can Serbia be called an "aggressor" while defending against alleged "rebellious victims—the KLA or Kosovo Liberation Army?"

Citizen Millick drew the analogy in Serbia to Waco. In Waco, armed citizens were "suspected" of harboring ill will against the government; in Serbia its armed immigrants claimed a land that "never has and never will belong to them."

Yeltsin vehemently voiced objections to U. S. led air strikes on Serbia wrote McMahon and Sly. He said, "Morally, we are above America." His foreign minister accused the U. S. of imposing its political-military-economic dictates on the world.

Russian protestations were likely political bombast to allay fellow Slavs and Milosevic since it required U. S.—European financial aid, energy and food. About 2,000 protesters swarmed near the U. S. Embassy in Moscow and "peacefully" burned the American flag, hurled eggs, bottles, ink and invectives.

China supported Milosevic and called for a halt to air strikes. It blamed the conflict on armed Albanian terrorists. China asserted, "Serbia has the legitimate power to crack down on terrorists."

"The Western powers, led by the U. S. had over-reacted in their meddling in other nations' affairs," wrote China's People's Daily.

India, Vietnam, Iraq and Indonesia criticized the bombings. Overall, "nations representing over one-half the world's population opposed the air strikes."

Other Criticisms of Clinton's War

Shaffer likened the "original dove to hawk" transformation of Clinton's attack on Serbia to LBJ's intervention in Vietnam. Clinton preached that containment of the war in Serbia was necessary, else "neighboring" countries like Albania, Macedonia, Greece and Turkey would become involved due to the "fleeing refugees," i. e., the domino effect.

Clinton and Johnson used the rationalizations of "credibility at stake, fighting for future generations, less cost now than later, fictional vital national interests, action is better than inaction and a free and democratic country as justifications" for interdiction. Most of the empty slogans, reasons and rationalizations were bogus, ludicrous and nonsensical when Johnson uttered them—just as they were when Clinton mouthed them.

Con artist Clinton, of course, ignored "ethnic cleansing" of the Kurds by Turkey, genocide in Indonesia, genocide in Rwanda and elsewhere in Africa as long as Serbia was neutralized in Kosovo. Shaffer concluded his column by saying that, except for the communist issue, Clinton's stance akin to that of Johnson, was not to be believed.

Citizen Drewe thought that Clinton's bombardment of Serbia was a diversion from China's stealing U. S. nuclear secrets and from the White House cover-up. He was quite cognizant that Clinton had bombed four countries (Sudan, Afghanistan, Iraq and Serbia) during the past seven months, "immediately after revelations of sexual or political misadventures became public."

Drewe wrote that NATO violated international law by attacking a sovereign nation. He also observed that the U. S. had no national interest in Serbia or was it vital to protect fictional U. S. interests in Kosovo.

According to Drewe, "The air strikes were a diversion to cover misdeeds of the Clinton administration."

Serbia's clever strategy may prolong NATO's mission according to Williams. Serbia's hides anti-aircraft missiles, disperses troops, moves frequently and attacks the Albanian rebels with small units. They shut off their radar defenses that protect positions of surface-to-surface missile sites, tactics that do not permit the enemy to "home in." A "hot" radar picture is necessary for enemy aircraft to zero in on selected targets.

Serbia defended itself from seven warships, 400 "NATO" planes and orbiting JSTARS, Rivet Joint and AWACS surveillance aircraft that senses, tracks and directs aircraft to targets. It does so by an elaborate bunker system, underground communications and an air base built under the mountain at Slatina.

They have an estimated 70 SA-7 mobile rocket launchers with back up, re-loading, 1,000 anti aircraft missiles—many shoulder fired, and many small weapons. The Serbian troops stay close to the rebels as protection thereby increasing civilian deaths, injuries and damage known in propaganda circles as "collateral damage."

Lynch considered the comparison of Milosevic to Hitler "a stretch." According to historians, Milosevic was not an imperialistic, head of a first rate power, one who protected a shrinking not an expanding country and one who had no "One World uber alles" design unlike imperialists Hitler and Clinton. "The Serbs were responding to Kosovar rebels who desired independence and were willing to fight for it," said Georgetown's Professor Winters.

Former ambassador to Croatia, Galbreath, said that Clinton's designation of Kosovo as a "power keg" was overstated. Conflicting territorial intentions in the Balkans by powerful European nations was not a part of the Kosovo problem.

Day Two of air strikes against Serbia continued while NATO defiantly escalated its attacks against the KLA wrote Clines. NATO commander, General Clark, vowed the air strikes would continue to "systematically and aggressively attack, disrupt, degrade, devastate and ultimately destroy enemy forces until Milosevic capitulated." The bombardment was aimed at decimating military targets, depots and factories that underpin Serbia's war machine.

Milosevic wasn't then ready to "give in." Meanwhile, thousands of Serb sympathizers protested outside the U. S. Embassy in Skopje. General Clark still planned to eliminate Milosevic's ability to make war, allow him to remain in power and observe the "imposed" peace pact. He dismissed Russian threats as a "terrible mistake."

Responses to Criticisms of Clinton's War

Clinton's "One World appointee echoes" Albright, Berger and Cohen backed up Clinton's declaration that included its "long term interests." Berger denied plans to commit U. S. ground forces or that a precedent had been set to intervene in a civil war. "Sovereignty" was considered to be a weak Serbian argument since its involvement in Croatia, Bosnia and Slovenia. He added that our involvement "thwarts the spread of hostilities and touted moral and other humanitarian values."

A CBS-Gallup poll of Americans revealed 41 percent opposed and 46 percent supported Clinton's air strikes, while 52 percent said peace in Yugoslavia was not worth American lives. Only 33 percent supported "peace in Yugoslavia."

Senators McConnell and Lieberman proposed $2.5 billion to "arm and train" Kosovars, but their proposal was met with "stunned silence" at the globally oriented White House.

On Day Three, two MIGs flying over Bosnia, were shot down by two U. S. F-15C pilots reported Clines and Myers. Military bunkers for the military hierarchy plus army and police outposts in Kosovo were included as targets.

The column related that Milosevic stripped autonomy away from the Kosovars in 1989. The Albanians had been waging an aggressive campaign for self-rule, although Kosovo had been a sacred province of Serbia for centuries. With reports of increased atrocities, NATO would strike at more army and police units situated in Kosovo.

Clinton broadcast the usual war propaganda to the Serbian people that Milosevic was "exposing you to violence and instability, diminishing your country's standing, isolating you from the rest of Europe and forcing your sons to keep fighting in a senseless conflict he could have prevented." Clinton also warned Milosevic that any evidence of ethnic cleansing atrocities in Kosovo would be turned over to the War Crimes International Tribunal or WCIT.

The Republican slate of presidential aspirants expressed their opinions about the air strikes. McCain, Elizabeth Dole, Forbes and Alexander favored them, while Quayle, Kasich, Smith, Bauer and Buchanan opposed. Bush didn't declare, but supported the troops. Mrs. Dole conceded the president's actions "might" contribute to a peaceful solution.

Hundreds of ordinary Russians were voluntarily lining up for military service to fight NATO on the side of the Serbs wrote Filipov. Inanely, they thanked Yugoslavia and Milosevic for keeping NATO from occupying Russia!

Meanwhile, Russia expelled NATO's representative in Moscow, called for charges against NATO that planned the bombing and sent two powerful warships to sea. The "largely for show" reactions were merely symbolic since Russia was seeking a $4.8 billion loan from the International Monetary Fund, IMF.

Day 4 reported one U. S. F-117 stealth fighter was shot down wrote Broder. The pilot was rescued by an elite "search and rescue" team within six hours. Each F-117 costs $43 million, about the cost of Clinton's impeachment and trial. The U. S. feared the loss of secret technology to the enemy that prevents radar detection. Its outer material absorbs radar signals, thus provides no echoes to Serbian air missile defense sites. It was probable that Russia could benefit from F-117's technology.

The U. S. and NATO expanded the target spectrum to include army troops and police forces in response to increased execution, deportation and forced marches of Albanian Kosovars.

Broder wrote that NATO saw a need for a change in strategy from bombing military targets to field troops and police because the Serbs were engaged in "ethnic cleansing atrocities." The change in strategy, however, stopped short of sending in ground forces.

Council of Foreign Relations senior fellow and dedicated global government proponent, Kupchan, viciously labeled Milosevic the "center of twisted nationalist ideologies and virulent nationalism" that propelled Yugoslavia into war. He favored the need for ground forces to strip Serbia of Kosovo.

Globalist Kupchan wanted Clinton to "prepare the American people for troop involvement, spread of war and threat to national security." Polls, however, strongly revealed that America was opposed to U. S. troop involvement. Kupchan was formerly on the staff of the National Security Council during Clinton's first term; thus it was "understandable" that his comments were in keeping with Clinton's one-world policies.

NATO critics did not believe that continued bombings would "spread the war south and incite calls for independence" by Albanians in Macedonia. Further, Yugoslavia was a sovereign country and NATO had no right to intervene under the charter of the UN. Clever, conniving, crafty Clinton, C^4, and NATO bypassed the UN Security Council in order to intervene in Serbia because "he couldn't obtain its permission." (The veto threats of Russia and China probably stood in the way!)

As expected, globalist Kupchan dismissed all arguments by critics because the "spread of war jeopardized U. S. security!" He was opposed to "nationalist myth-making;" hence, nationalist Serbia must be neutralized.

Kupchan wanted ground troops to silence Milosevic, independence for Kosovo and removal of Milosevic from power. (It appeared that Kupchan was bent simply on "destroying national sovereignty worldwide" with the U. S. included and setting another international meddling precedent for foreign entanglements under any 'legal pretense' that included human rights, peace, spread of war and related.")

The author felt scant doubt remained that meddling in the internal affairs of sovereign nations while denouncing nationalism globally and selling out U. S. sovereignty in the process were Clinton's primary objectives in foreign policy. Recent foreign entanglements abetted by mainly U. S. forces with token assistance rendered from other nations began with the Korean War and continued during the Vietnam War. Interventionist policy was more recently implemented with "practice run" invasions, missile and/or conventional bombings in efforts at implementation and/or denationalization by armed forays against relatively weak foreign nations like Grenada, Panama, Somalia, Haiti, Bosnia, Sudan, Iraq, Afghanistan and Serbia.

Clinton's "Quick Air Strike Strategy" Failure

After three days of bombardment, Apple wrote that the strategy to bring Milosevic to his knees, accept the peace pact and allow NATO forces in Kosovo, had failed. Clinton mistakenly thought his "quick air strike strategy" would deter more atrocities inflicted by Serbians on Albanians in Kosovo.

All NATO nations were opposed to sending troops into Serbia. The U. S. public polls revealed a similar reluctance to sending troops. Nevertheless, NATO then planned a wider campaign to bomb Serbian tanks, artillery and ground troops. Having traveled that road before with the Nazis, Serbia countered that plan with immediate dispersal of troops, armaments, defenses and supplies.

Wright's column discussed the real issue at hand was not the immediate bombings, but the beginning of intervention over a nation's human rights record. It could set precedence for intervening "contrary" to two broad provisions in the UN Charter, which were to restrict the use of force only for reasons of "individual or collective self defense and at flash points that threatened international peace and security." The two provisions were not applicable to Kosovo. By intervention in Serbia, "human rights superseded the right of a nation's sovereignty and non-interference!" Wright correctly surmised that such a precedent could be "applicable anywhere in the world."

Issues like genocide led to U. S. involvement in Somalia, Haiti, Bosnia-Herzegovina and by the Kurds in Northern Iraq. The stakes in Kosovo appeared applicable globally. The crux of the matter in Kosovo was whether a large "minority" population of Albanian Muslims, dominated by Serbian Orthodox Christians, reserved the "right" to participate politically in Europe, a region ruled by Judeo-Christian values.

Ex Congression Hamilton said, "The cost and dangers in Kosovo are far too high—far beyond what our national interests dictate" and "supporting Kosovar Albanians and their quest for independence has implications for nations with substantial ethnic groups within."

Ironically, the U. S. "supported" Turkey in its resistance to a Kurdish movement for autonomy and independence within its borders. "The notion that you can bomb a sovereign nation to change its mind has not yet been proven," said Scowcroft.

Citizen Wasserman labeled Clinton the "Warrior Prince" and asked that he "keep us out of Kosovo's civil war—just like you kept yourself out of Vietnam."

Wasserman drew the analogy between Kosovo, province of Serbia and its ethnic Albanians who wanted autonomy and independence. The UN intervenes, sides with the rebel Albanians and bombs Serbia.

Now substitute California, a state in the United States, inundated with Hispanics with factions that covet autonomy and independence. Wasserman asked, "Does the UN side with the Hispanics, and Does Clinton bomb California into compliance?" He added that this scenario shouldn't be too difficult even for a Rhodes scholar dropout to understand?

Citizen Williams accused Clinton of "unconstitutionally" using the U. S. military by placing our troops under UN command. Citizen Williams perceived that the "terrorists and drug traffickers" of the Kosovo Liberation Army, KLA, would benefit most.

Williams advised Congress to" halt the usurpation of power and demand that all U. S. troops be brought home and we withdraw from the United Nations."

Another citizen, Bozic, observed that our "fair-minded media" splashed "Albanian deaths" across the front page, while "Serbian deaths" were barely noticed and usually buried in Section D, page 26. He did not view the war as freedom or liberation, but as a "mob of people trying to seize part of a country to join their own." Bozic added, "They do not wave a Kosovar Liberation flag, but an Albanian flag!"

Schmitt wrote that draft dodger Clinton honored the bravery and skill of an elite, "search and rescue" helicopter team that rescued the pilot of a downed F-117 stealth fighter from behind enemy lines. The pilot had parachuted to earth and fortunately only suffered bruises and a battered kneecap.

While NATO stepped up its air bombardment, Kosovar Albanian refugees were streaming into Albania and Macedonia and incurring violent demonstrations against the American Embassy wrote Kifner. Most refugees were women and children and the whereabouts of their men were unknown.

NATO continued its bombardment against Serbia but rejected the use of ground troops or arming Kosovars scribed Thomma and Parker. Military targets in Kosovo were expanded from the previous list. American jets strafed Serbian troops whenever spotted.

Meanwhile relief workers attempted to aid fleeing Albanian refugees. Reports of Albanian men separated from their families being tortured were rife.

Albright denied reports that air strikes increased the numbers of atrocities, motivated refugees to flee and "hastened an ethnically cleansed Kosovo." Her limp retort was, "Milosevic was planning to do so anyway."

NATO was still trying to locate and destroy Serbia's air missile defense. It also focused on widely publicizing its "humanitarian" justification for intervention.

Clinton thought that air strikes alone would pound Serbia into submission
Felt massive damage inflicted would result in a successful mission
 Find and destroy their air missile defense,
 Bomb at will without lingering suspense,
And justify their "humane war" that puts Serbia out of commission

Serbia didn't want to grant Kosovo autonomy or separation
Since the province of Kosovo is part of the sovereign Serbian nation
 The Kosovar-Serb mix was 80 to 20,
 Disproportionate in nature, more than plenty
So Serbia embarked on an "ethnic cleansing" new policy operation

Citizen Goldenfeld called Clinton's assault on Serbia a flagrant shameful act of aggression because they had not attacked any other nation, a neighbor, U. S. ally or even U. S. International Borders were not crossed. Serbia was merely putting down a secessionist rebellion—a civil war akin to Russia and Chechnya, Sri Lanka and the Tamil rebels and Turkey's suppression of Kurds. (He might have added the U. S. "North vs. the South" civil war.)

In plain language, a sovereign country cannot commit aggression within its own borders. He called the Clinton administration "trigger-happy." Clinton had bombed four countries including Sudan, Afghanistan, Iraq and Serbia illegally and immorally in the past seven months. According to Goldenfeld, Clinton's tactics made the U. S. the "planetary bully."

Citizen Guyer accused the Clinton administration of using "trade" as the ultimate objective to justify bombing Kosovo and turning over the

Long Beach Naval Base to China's COSCO. If trade was the ultimate objective, he asked, "Why bomb Yugoslavia's automobile factory?"

> Citizen Innerarity said Clinton bombed Serbia in violation
> Of the UN Security Council—"bypassed" without justification
>> KLA was doing its level "best"
>> From Serbia, province Kosovo wrest,
> As Clinton sided with the rebels to weaken Serbia, "sovereign nation"

Chapter 3

Clinton's "Instant Solution" War Strategy Fails

Clinton gambled on an "instant solution" war strategy that obviously failed. This failure caused an overload of propaganda that featured inflammatory issues of increased genocide, crimes against humanity, fleeing refugees and related emotional appeals to stir public sympathy for continuing the air strikes.

Further details are described chronologically under Air Strikes Fail after One Week—Milosevic Still Defiant, Assorted Reactions to the "Instant Solution" Strategy Failure, Brookman's Analysis of the "Instant Solution" Strategy Failure, Thompson Makes a Case for Clinton's War, Continuance and Enlargement of the U. S. Led NATO Forces, Mead's Speculations about Clinton's War, Author's Perception of the Situation, More Criticisms of the War by Citizens et al. Revision of the Refugee Dilemma and Further Expansion of Air Bombardment, Madeline's Morass and Reactions, Decision to Widen the War and Reactions and Albanian Imperialistic Dreams. Other topics are interspersed among the main headings.

Air Strikes Fail after One Week—Milosevic Still Defiant

Inasmuch as the bombardment had failed to bring Milosevic down after one week of intense air bombardment, NATO stepped up its "emotionally appealing laments about increased genocide" rather than "destruction of Serbia's military capability" wrote Clines. Hordes of refugees were fleeing to Albania, Macedonia and Montenegro to compound the people displacement problem.

Failure of U. S. led NATO bombings had forced a shift in strategy to maintain public support in the U. S., which was heretofore minimal. "Crimes against humanity are increasing," said Rubin, State Department voice. British Foreign Secretary Cook said that refugees were being herded to "concentration areas" somewhat reminiscent of herded refugees in Bosnia subsequently executed by Serbs. (They were not sent to gas chambers or incinerators, however.) NATO officials denounced Milosevic for waging a "scorched earth" campaign to maintain power, while it "hypocritically" decimated Serbia with air bombardment to attain "mini U. S.—European global power."

Pentagon's Bacon foolishly commented that the Serb's military and special police dispersed into small units making their "mass" destruction well nigh impossible. (Did he logically expect them to "sit still and pose as willing mass targets in a war situation?")

Whitney's account of NATO's apparent dejection after pounding Serbia for a week with cruise missiles, smart bombs, stealth planes, high-tech bombers and other state-of-the-art weapons with a still defiant, unyielding Milosevic was "discompooperating" to Clinton and company and not proceeding according to White House power-mad desires to say the least. The basic strategy that devastating air power would quickly achieve its goal was "fatally flawed."

(A reasonable explanation is possible if one ponders seriously that "conventional" air strikes are not equivalent to the complete devastation of an "atomic bomb" drop. Perhaps that is the parallel analogy on which White House planners based their faulty strategy. Additionally, military land forces are inevitably required to secure the devastated territory from the effects of either "conventional or atomic bombing.")

The attacks also failed to halt "ethnic cleansing" in Kosovo; on the contrary, the exodus escalated and revealed that "ultra nationalist" Milosevic was no push over. He offered to negotiate if the bombings stopped, but NATO rejected that proposal outright. (Apparently, inflated egos of Clinton and cohorts in NATO were at stake.)

Assorted Reactions to the "Instant Solution" Strategy

According to NATO's Solana, "Ground forces would only invade Serbia if peace was negotiated and peace keepers were needed. Albanians in Kosovo and Serbs who ruled over Kosovo would have to agree as well." The imposed peace agreement would grant autonomy to Kosovo under Serbian rule for a three-year transition period

Three Los Angeles area citizens expressed their views regarding the situation in Kosovo. Citizen Cook questioned why the inert, demolished "carcass" of the crashed stealth fighter, F-117, was not immediately vaporized to preserve its secrets!

Citizen Maurer drew analogies between Los Angeles Mayor Riordan and Milosevic by just interchanging a few words. Riordan: "We act to prevent a wider secession (war) of the San Fernando Valley from Los Angeles)." Los Angeles (Allied) forces expected a tough, dangerous fight." "Milosevic (Riordan) employed radio addresses to blast secession." It seemed obvious that both Milosevic and Riordan wanted to retain their respective territories –Serbia's province of Kosovo and Los Angeles' San Fernando Valley.

Citizen Boer felt that the present situation in Serbia was like riding in a bus with a drunk driver at the wheel.

While air strikes continued around the clock, clever conciliator Clinton threatened Milosevic with U. S. and international support for Kosovo's independence rather than autonomy, if he didn't sign the peace treaty wrote Kornblut. He accused Milosevic of systematically expelling the Albanians from Serbia.

Milosevic wanted the bombing to cease first, but Clinton rejected that want. Italy's Prime Minister D'Alena and Britain's Prime Minister Blair supported Clinton.

Russia's Primakov repeated the charge that Clinton's air strikes were a clear violation of the UN Security Council and its charter when it commenced air strikes.

In Athens, 6,000 protesters demonstrated outside the U. S. Embassy and burned U. S. and British flags. Similar demonstrations also occurred in Spain and Bosnia.

Parker, Donnelly and Demick wrote that U. S. Blackhawk and British helicopters searched for three missing U. S. soldiers "possible abducted" from Macedonia. The soldiers were on reconnaissance while driving a Humvee approximately three miles from the Serbian border.

Clinton planned to continue his strategy of "more steel and determination" to succeed. New targets including government building in Belgrade were being considered. Notwithstanding, NATO's General Clark was "not convinced" that more air strikes would stop the exodus of Albanians from Serbia.

At the same time, Clinton was drawing additional support from Carlucci, ex secretary of defense, to send troops into the fracas.

NATO's Shea commented that the Serbs were systematically destroying Kosovo's archives including property deeds, marriage licenses, birth certificates and related records, evidence to deny the Albanians ever lived in Kosovo.

Russia prepared to send seven warships to the Mediterranean and would not hesitate to use nukes against a potential foe penned Filipov.

The imminent deployment of warships would ensure Russia's security whenever the Defense Ministry considered it necessary.

Russia objected to the "precedent" set by "trigger-happy" Clinton. Foreign Minister Ivanov called the air strikes a "barbarous aggression against Yugoslavia" and "reports of ethnic cleansing were simply an American propaganda campaign."

Palmer's column indicated that political support for sending ground forces to Kosovo was growing. Senator Hagel, ex Defense Secretary Carlucci, ex ambassador Abramovitz and Senator McCain encouraged the use of ground troops to "insure successful attainment of objectives—peace, stability and the return of refugees to Kosovo."

Thomma wrote that Clinton warned Milosevic he would be held responsible for the safety of three captured U. S. soldiers and that "there was no basis for their capture." Before capture, Ramizez, Stone and Gonzalez were heard to say, "They were under fire…we are surrounded." Clinton expected them to be treated according to the rules of the Geneva Convention.

Since the Yugoslavian Embassy in Washington, D. C. closed one week ago, the U. S. planned to work for their release through the Swedish Embassy.

NATO's Solana said NATO remained unified and resolved to stay the course as its tactics hastened "ethnic cleansing" in Kosovo. He also "challenged" reports that NATO could not stop ethnic cleansing in time.

A bridge over the Danube River was destroyed and disrupted both military and civilian movement of goods wrote Myers and Becker. Another bridge that connected Novi Sad was left intact. General Clark, however, did not rule out destroying the second bridge—weather permitting.

Amid confusing circumstances surrounding capture of three American soldiers, the Pentagon didn't think they should be considered "prisoners of war!" (Then why did Clinton want them treated according to "rules of war" according to the Geneva Convention?)

General Clark, NATO commander, also said that more "civilian" structures with minimal military use were being targeted including "routes" throughout Yugoslavia." Although NATO repeatedly asserted they "had" the forces to wage war on Yugoslavia, the number of aircraft involved in the war were constantly being increased. Five B-1 bombers, 13 F-117 stealth fighters, the destroyer USS Ross and the cruiser USS Vella Gulf were augmenting present forces. The aircraft carrier, USS Theodore Roosevelt, was also buttressing the war assault.

Meanwhile, the Serbs were busy rounding up the remaining stragglers of the Kosovo Liberation Army.

It appeared that more "NATO" fighting forces were required, the KLA was in the throes of elimination and ethnic cleansing was proceeding at mach speed due to acceleration and widespread air attacks.

Brookman's Analysis of the "Instant Solution" Strategy Failure

Bookman's description of U. S. involvement in Kosovo to date (April 1, 1999) was labeled as a failure despite mythical high-sounding strategy, diplomacy and political hot air. He drew a parallel between "America fighting for independence, not subjugation under England" and " Serbs fighting for nationhood, not subjugation under NATO."

He viewed America as "not standing by as a bully brutalizes a victim as we brutalize Yugoslavia while wearing a moral, white hat." Bookman noted the U. S. has obvious superiority in air power and technology, but the Serbs had "dedication and commitment."

Bookman perceived the U. S. as a "super nation captive to 'Global 911' to right injustice anywhere." The U. S. is driven by the "notion of our morality," recklessly goaded by the "immoral" man in the White House. Hopefully and wistfully Clinton's "moral" intervention may fail.

It may happen that "moral war" intervention might not work
Though the right thing was done, there does realistically lurk
  That the Serbs will remain resolute,
  Absorb all missile and bombs we shoot,
And force ground troop to be ordered by Clinton, "immoral dork"

Myers described how predominantly U. S. aircraft and cruise missiles continued the attack on Belgrade, which destroyed important centers of security forces and other military targets. Casualties were not mentioned. General Clark said there would be no sanctuary for Serbia's military leaders. Neither had ten days of bombing halted forced expulsion of Albanians from Kosovo.

Clinton remained determined to see the mission through. One World strategy would not tolerate a defeatist exit, stalemate or surcease. Despite bombing a military staging area in Kosovo, the Serbs's offensive in Kosovo plowed on despite Clinton's dogged determination.

Shenon's column cited the State Department was considering taking refugees "if only to encourage reluctant nations to do likewise." Such announcements are usually a precursor to actualization. Hopefully and later, the refugees would be "repatriated" to their non-existent homes.

In the interim, refugees would become wards of many European nations and the U. S. for "indefinite" periods. Germany suggested that Albanians stay in the Balkans. Congress had already imposed a ceiling of 78,000 refugees admitted from all nations to the U. S. this year.

Thompson Makes a Case for Clinton's War

Thompson's column made a case for U. S. involvement in Serbia. He cited peace in Bosnia, national interest, humanitarian responsibility and leadership in international organizations under the mantle of "collective security for peace." He though that "isolationism was dead." Thomson cited John Donne's statement, "No man is an island, entirely of itself;

every man is a piece of a continent, a part of the main…any man's death diminishes me, because I am involved in mankind, and therefore never seem to know for whom the bell tolls; it tolls for thee."

He tried to buttress his argument with victory in W. W. II and defeats in Vietnam and Somalia with the admonition that "we carry a special burden to help those nations it can help."

Thompson dismissed criticisms including lack of an exit strategy, another Vietnam stalemate, a civil war, insurmountable country and no abiding national interest. Critics pointed out that Nazi bombing of Britain, bombing of North Vietnam and bombing of Iraq did not force capitulation. In fact, the collective spirits of those enemy nations were revived to resist with increased resolve.

Columnist Thompson thrust all criticisms aside for commitment to saving the lives and property of Albanians in Kosovo. He haughtily opined, "It was our duty to sacrifice and the price we pay for a better world."

Continuance and Enlargement of the U. S. Led NATO Forces

Myers' column reported that a second bridge spanning the Danube in Novi Sad and a rail line from Bosnia had been destroyed. It was the fulfillment of General Clark's previous hope—weather permitting. General Clark also requested, "with NATO's approval," that Apache helicopter gun ships and 2,000 solders be sent to seek out and destroy armor.

On this 11th day, the U. S. led NATO mission then had two missions: military and humanitarian. Defense Secretary Cohen ordered 11 ships now in the U. S. naval armada, 13 more F-117s and 5 B-1 bombers to the Serbian Civil War zone. As expected in any UN operation, embarrassing, pitiful contributions by other NATO nations were not revealed. At the same time, delivery of food, tents, sleeping bags and cots for use by refugees were being air lifted to Macedonia.

As the refugee problem in Kosovo escalated, NATO planned to send 6,000 to 8,000 troops to Albania to render humanitarian assistance scribed Dahlburg and Shogren. An estimated 765,000 Kosovars had been displaced since March. If the pace continued, Kosovo may well be ethnically cleansed in two or three weeks. Apparently "U. S.—NATO bombing had worked only too well!

Macedonia was at its peak ability to render assistance amid fear that water, food and sanitation might be strained. It then sheltered 120,000 refugees with more expected—hopefully re-directed to other countries.

Serbs were still committing atrocities in Kosovo. NATO continued to bomb mercilessly infrastructure and military targets like bridges, railways, depots and buildings. The U. S., British, French, Italian and German governments had agreed that any peace pact must provide for the return of refugees to Yugoslavia under escort by NATO's peace keeper troops.

Clinton planned to continue widespread bombing. Simultaneously, military and civilian aircraft would ferry food and supplies to the refugees. Germany, Ireland and the U. S. were willing to accept some refugees. Clinton "might" ease already lax immigration policies to accommodate more refugees.

General Clark requested the USS Theodore Roosevelt aircraft carrier and the 24 Apache gun ships be used against the Serbs in Kosovo.

Russia protested that NATO's attacks were engaged in a "ruthless war of extermination" against Yugoslavia. It threatened to withdraw its 400 "peacekeepers" in Bosnia. The Bolsheviks have been traditional religious, ethnic and political allies with Yugoslavia, but urgently needed the West's dollars and political support. Logically, any Russian protest and bluster were mainly "for show."

Mead's Speculations about Clinton's War

Council of Foreign Relations, senior fellow Mead, labeled the Rape of Kosovo, Bay of Pigs and Fall of Saigon as the worst foreign policy flops since W. W. II. Clinton's massive bombing were expected to protect the Albanians in Kosovo, weaken Milosevic, buttress NATO, stabilize the Balkans, tout the sagacity of Clinton's foreign policy and assure the safety of U. S. group troops.

Instead, ethnic cleansing was almost completed, Milosevic remained strong, NATO faced an internal crisis, and Albania, Macedonia and surrounding Kosovo were in turmoil. Clinton's credibility as a foreign policy expert was shattered with shame and guilt and three U. S. soldiers had been captured.

"Pundit" Mead viewed the Yugoslavian situation as a complete mess. Mead charged that long range contingency plans in case of military-political setbacks were ill or never considered. He anticipated either use of ground forces or arming Serbia's neighbors and partitioning Kosovo as undesirable options. A build up of a politically costly and honorable invasion force was preferred but not expected from Clinton.

"Seer" Mead surmised that unless the Serbs were forced out of Kosovo, refugees returned and set up in an independent Kosovo, NATO would suffer. He envisioned the need to arm the Croats, Bosnian, Muslims and Albanians in a war of revenge against the hated Serbs. NATO needed this victory to sustain itself, the rule of law and as defender of Europe's collective security.

The remainder of the article was a fantastic rumination of pure speculation along with unrealistically arming Serb haters. "Soothsayer" Mead's erroneous predictions were based on "if, might and maybe," i. e., purely speculative possibilities.

Schmitt surmised that the 8,000 NATO troops and 24 Apaches operated by U. S. regulars might be the vanguard of an invasion force. The White House denied this latter contention. Apache gun ships are ground support helicopters designed to destroy tanks, defenses and related. In any case, the air strikes had thus far failed to destroy the Serbian war machine especially in Kosovo.

Clinton needed obsequious "permission" from NATO leaders to send the Apaches to Kosovo. The Apache has 16 laser-guided Hellfire missiles with three-mile attack capability, operate in an eight-helicopter pack and blast a path through the enemy. Apache helicopters are "all weather" weaponry with one exception—not under "dense fog" conditions. They are also vulnerable to small arms fire and shoulder-fired missiles.

On the 12th night of air strikes wrote John, NATO forces bombed an Army headquarters, ammo plant, oil refineries and other targets in Belgrade, Novi Sad and Pristina as the KLA was preparing its final defense. At the same time, U. S. troops were busy installing and manning a multiple Launch Rocket System in Macedonia to fire missiles into Serbia.

Yugoslav's ambassador to the UN, Jovonic, said that Belgrade still remained defiant and the attacks only "increased our resolve in defending our country."

True to Clinton's past selective "personal crisis" bombings on carefully selected nations and accommodating the displaced, the U. S. would shelter 20,000 Albanian refugees in Guantanamo and Guam. A coordinated airlift would be instituted for transferring more refugees to other European nations like Germany, Turkey and elsewhere.

General Clark called the Serbian move to destabilize Macedonia and force NATO to deal with the numerous refugees a deliberate strategy. He admitted air attacks had not alleviated the refugee exodus fiasco and NATO was preoccupied with airlifting supplies and resettling the displaced.

British Lieutenant General Jackson, commander of 10,000 troops in Macedonia, had been directed to render humanitarian assistance. The influx of refugees forced Macedonia to close its borders, but "borderless" State Department's Strobe Talbot urged it to re-open them—which it did.

The 13th day of air attacks on Serbia was intensified during perfect weather conditions on 27 mainly unspecified targets in Nis and Novi Sad, although a power station and an oil refinery were identified. Clinton promised relentless bombing would continue "until we prevail and ethnic cleansing in Kosovo cannot stand as a permanent event."

Albananian officials objected to Clinton's plan of airlifting refugees to foreign countries because it would only further Milosevic's goal of ridding them from the region.

In order for the bombing to cease, Clinton demanded that Milosevic withdraw forces from Kosovo, permit refugees to return and allow NATO peacekeepers into Kosovo. Clinton's British echo, Prime Minister Blair, reverberated "uber alles" Clinton's sentiments. Clinton did admit that although Milosevic precipitated the refugee crisis, the U. S. along with other nations' token air bombardment escalated the Albanian refugee situation in Kosovo.

Clinton ordered massive air bombardment on Serbian soil
With hopes Milosevic would soon capitulate and recoil
    A rapid surrender to NATO was planned,
    But Serbia fought fiercely for its homeland,
Which caused the refugee problem to reach a vaporous boil

Clinton was counseled on Serbian-Kosovo policy by three "devisors"
Albright, Bergen and Cohen, the troika of one-world oriented "advisers"
    Negotiations had failed miserably,
    Clinton was committed inextricably,
And fingers would point at "who is to blame" by our trio of global "revisers"

Clinton gave "demands" to Milosevic that equated to outright capitulation
Serbian police and troops must first withdraw from Kosovo in shameful subjugation
    Give Kosovo a Muslim "state-autonomy,"
    As an act toward "Euro global hegemony,"
Accept NATO "peace keepers" to return safely refugees to "their NATO formed nation"

Author's Perception of the Situation

The recent "practice nation meddling exercises of 'mini' invasions against mainly weak and hapless nations" began in Grenada and continued with Panama, Somalia, Haiti, Bosnia, Iraq, Afghanistan and Sudan. Nation meddling still continues in Iraq. They were basically "trial meddling exercises in the internal affairs of sovereign nations" in relatively safe, varying degrees "to test domestic tolerance reactions from the public, media and globally educated, brainwashed U. S. students and foreign responses from other nations to establish a continuum of precedents."

The one world zealots astutely observed the relatively meager absence of intense domestic dismay and international outcry, thus became more emboldened. Accordingly, striking while the iron was hot, the one-world proponents now led by chief sovereign nation meddler, Clinton, ventured into the most serious nation meddling challenge to date—Serbia. Serbia's importance was crucial toward establishing a "mini one-world Europe" through the use of a new U. S.—NATO "offensive" for further nation meddling operations.

Serbia turned out to be somewhat of a "miscalculation." Massive air bombardment failed to bring defiant, militant, nationalistic Milosevic to his knees in "instant, abject surrender" as planned. Clinton's trio of sycophantic advisors (Albright, Berger and Cohen) were willing A, B and C echoes and accomplices of his strategy. It appeared unlikely that "what if or Plan B options" were ever seriously considered.

Therefore, the underlying reason for unconditional surrender was to set a precedent for "legal," global intervention by the "Globocops" in any sovereign nation under any pretext including internal strife, human rights violations, humanitarian concerns, democracy, nation building and global peace—whether requested or not. Serbia was a fierce, European, nationalist sovereign nation whose resistance to "mini U. S.—European one world order" imposition must be mercilessly defeated. To allow Serbia to emerge in defiance of "mini one word order imperialism" was unthinkable and would resound as an ignominious defeat of NATO, forceful military arm or "mechanic" of the United Nations. Clinton's alleged international leadership prowess would suffer greatly as well.

Clinton, NATO and the United Nations were amalgamated as one in relentless pursuit of denationalization, desovereignization and one world hegemony presided over by "appointees, tribunals and organizations in which not even one member had been 'directly selected or elected' by the populaces of the individual nations." Alas, if that objective ever eventuated, it would be the "mother of all international coups" to date—April 6, 1999.

More Criticisms of Clinton's War by Citizens et al.

Citizen Mulley said that the U. S. had no business meddling in the internal affairs of foreign nations. He asked thoughtfully, "Would the U. S. like to see foreign troop invading the U. S. on the pretext of solving our internal domestic problems?"

Mulley mused that if gutless politicians were not tied to Clinton's apron strings, maybe they'd have the "moxie" to impeach him for "abuse of power."

Citizen Mulley saw that Clinton couldn't keep his own house in order
Feigns to solve foreign nation problems beset with internal disorder
    Invasion of Somalia and Haiti were superficial,
    Air strikes in Sudan, Afghanistan, Iraq not beneficial,
Still "Globocop Bill" refuses to stop illegals at our "Mex" border

Millick, citizen, asked the public to imagine the Oklahoma City bombing a million times over to fully comprehend what Clinton has done to Iraq and Serbia. Five thousand children have died in Iraq, yet no one has accused the U. S. of genocide! Millick opined that the "U. S. acts like an unconscionable, war-mongering savage with a policy that 'might makes right.'"

Citizen Jansen wondered why Clinton, as a bible carrying Christian, failed to halt bombing on Christendom's three high holy days, Good Friday through Easter, even when requested by the Pope. Yet, he heeded the Muslim's request not to bomb Iraq on Ramadan, their high holy period. Jansen asked, "Is this an ethnic double standard or what? Clinton is a hideous hypocrite."

Kifner's column described ethnic Albanians continuing to flee Kosovo to Albania despite

Milosevic's declaration of "cease fire." Many refused to go back because they have no homes and nothing to eat. Others didn't trust the Serbian police who asked for money as the price for saving a child's life or their own. Others had witnessed massacres and were very frightened.

Gore spoke to Primakov and asked for Russia's help in mediating a diplomatic solution wrote Perlez. Primakov was rebuffed at a previous attempt to negotiate peace. "Statesman" Gore said that he "preferred" diplomacy to bombing.

According to Schmitt, NATO rejected Milosevic's call for a "cease fire" on Easter; instead, it chose to escalate its "fair weather" air bombardment. Unbelievably, compassionate White House echo, Defense Secretary Cohen, called the offer "not only completely unacceptable but absurd." Bombing targets were focused on the corridor near the Kosovo-Albanian border known as the "kill box." One errant missile hit an apartment building.

American warplanes destroyed four separate bridges and other targets in Kosovo. NATO justified destroying the infrastructure (bridges, buildings, factories and related) because they supplied essential goods to the military and police forces. British Air Commander Wilby predicted the air strikes would soon severely disrupt the Serbian offensive.

The White House announced that Yugoslavian ships would be barred from U. S. ports and territorial waters. It also revealed that commercial airlines were hired to fly 20,000 refugees to Guantanamo, Cuba.

Charen's column cited Senator Lugar as saying, "We are losing the war." Charen asked, "Did any one declare war?" She didn't believe the White House assertion they were aware "bombing would speed up ethnic cleansing." She thought bombing was intended to "save" Kosovo from ethnic cleansing and brutality. Otherwise, "Where was the humanitarian plan or was it just an after thought?"

Charen doubted displaced Kosovars could return to see their homes again or a "free and democratic" Kosovo as fantasized by Albright would result.

She also asked why the credibility of the U. S. and NATO weren't at stake when Croatia drove 150,000 Serbs from their homes amid torture, murder, rape and disfigurement. "Wasn't the timing ripe?" Perhaps the credibility of the U. S. and NATO were not at stake then! (Perhaps Clinton's personal problems were not then in a "crisis" stage.)

Charen did not call the displacement of Albanians from Kosovo "genocide," since they weren't transported by boxcars to concentration camps for lethal gassing in ovens.

Cypriot, acting president of Cyprus, planned to fly to Belgrade in hopes of persuading Milosevic to release three POWs as a "good will gesture" reported Cabrera and Proyen. Vivian Ramirez, mother of Staff Sergeant Andrew was elated and prepared to fly to Cyprus to meet him. The DOD and the U. S. Army would provide escort. Vivian and husband were placed on standby, ready to fly to Germany.

The Pentagon said the prospective release of POWs would have no effect on continued bombardment. Gore even called Vivian Ramirez to console her and to give her optimism.

Milosevic declared the crisis was over, the KLA was defeated, negotiations for acceptable peace with ethnic Albanians were underway, refugees could return and no reason existed for NATO to continue bombing; however, NATO rejected the offer. Russia urged NATO to at least consider it.

Erlanger viewed the peace proposal strategy as a ruse to divide NATO members. Pentagon's Bacon called the peace offer a ploy intended to affect public opinion in Russia, Greece and Turkey. It was a sign of discomfiture. The U. S. wanted Russia's help to negotiate an acceptable solution and to end air bombardment "before" NATO's birthday at end of March 1999.

Citizen Legg reminded the public that the civil war in Kosovo was started by the KLA against Serbia's government with the "intent of separation." Rather than highlighting this fundamental fact, the globally oriented White House "chose" to feature genocide, bombed churches, homeless refugees, starvation and "the children" to offset "one world" Clinton's recklessness and stupidity in ordering air bombardment.

Unlike the media, Legg proposed the obvious but crucial question, "If there was widespread 'genocide,' why aren't there hundreds of thousands of 'dead,' not live refugees?"

Legg also noted that Albania was a firm ally of the USSR at the time Marshal Tito denounced the communist policies of Stalin and his successors. Citizen Legg mused that it was about time that we had "balanced" reporting.

Revision of the Refugee Dilemna and Further Expansion of Air Bombardment

Columnist Becker described revised plans "not" to airlift Kosovo refugees from Macedonia and Guantanamo to the U. S. Instead, refugee barracks would be built in Albania. Some concerns had been raised about "upsetting Macedonia's ethnic balance!"

The White House bowed reluctantly to pressure groups and aid organizations even though it upset slightly their plans to suffuse America with more diversity. Macedonia stealthily and swiftly deported 45,000 refugees, about 9,500 to Albania in an overnight operation without informing refugee helpers. The operation kept refugees uninformed of their destination and caused many family separations. Albania was "willing to accept refugees as long as western nations housed, fed and provided for them."

Some relief agency representatives remarked that displacement from Kosovo was bad; moving them from the region was worse and transplanting them to Guantanamo was worst of all.

(Would American Second, arch hypocrite Clinton only evince some heartfelt concerns about upsetting "ethnic imbalance" in the U. S.? Are you nuts?)

Sowell questioned that a "clear-cut" reason never existed for our involvement in Kosovo. The

administration displayed no evidence of a real plan but merely "reacted to the moment," after Clinton realized the "three-day, quickie strategy and out" had failed miserably.

The "false" claim of a "national interest" was really spurious
That we sided with the Kosovars, made many people furious
    To give humanitarian aid is good,
    Bomb-Tomahawk air strikes never supply food,
And to spill our blood in a foreign civil war is inglorious

Serbia then resorted to using human shields to protect its factories and bridges, where they withstand the night and listen to rock music folk songs.

Kifner related that the Serbs secretly removed refugees from the Albanian border. No one seemed to know where the Albanians went. The border was not quiet and relief officials were mystified. The remainder of the column was conjectural.

One day after the Serbs closed the border to refugees they were replaced by tanks wrote Kifner. Soldiers were seen setting up artillery, mortars and positioning mines in trenches. It was obvious they were "digging in."

Relief officials still had no idea what happened to the missing refugees. As per Kifner's column, the U. S. had agreed to accept 20,000 refugees, Canada—6,000, Australia—4,000, Norway—6,000, Turkey—20,000 and Germany—10,000. Other nations promised to accept paltry numbers.

Erlanger said that NATO dismissed Milosevic's peace offering "out of hand;" bombings would continue. White House spokesman Crowley derided the accord as a "charm offer" negotiated between Milosevic and pacifist Albanian Rugova. Crowley said, "Words and propaganda are not enough."

Clinton's "mini one world European" price for a cease bombing included full political autonomy to Kosovo (nation building), withdrawal of part or all Serb forces from Kosovo (neutralize the enemy) and allow 30,000 NATO troops in to enforce an "imposed" peace (subjugate a Serbian province to NATO's control). In the process, it would maintain NATO's credibility and right to intervene in civil unrest.

Meanwhile, Serbs inhabited the bridges near Belgrade and the one remaining near Novi Sad that crossed the Danube.

Erlanger related how Cypriot leader, Kyprianou, failed to obtain the release of three American POWs from Milosevic. He blamed NATO for not halting the bombings; instead, they were intensified. A halt in air strikes would have been interpreted as a peaceful gesture. Unyielding NATO, however, preferred an "unconditional" release of the POWs.

Kyprianou added, "Even if the air strikes continued for 100 days, the rest of the world must understand that bombing would not solve the problem and this region needs peace based on justice and morality, peace based on freedom and respect of borders."

Seslj, Yugoslav deputy Prime Mminister, said, "Freedom for the soldiers is out of the question," because "the U. S. is leading in an undeclared war against Yugoslavia and should be tried as terrorists."

At the time, Serbia resorted to using human shields to protect its factories and bridges, where they endured the night by listening to rock music folk songs.

Citizen Felsman labeled Clinton and Blair as "two schoolboys playing at war," since neither has the foggiest idea of what it means to commit men to battle and death. Draft dodger Clinton avoided the Vietnam War and revisionist-like mistakenly asserted that W. W. II started in the

Balkans, an outright lie—since it commenced with Hitler's invasion of Eastern Europe.

Another citizen, Vaquer, viewed U. S. involvement in Serbia as inane because civil war hatreds hark back to 1300 A. D. He saw the war as another Vietnam quagmire and hoped this madness would end pronto.

Citizen Ulbrick perceived Clinton's air bombardment completely destroying Serbia's infrastructure. Reconstruction will follow, refugees will inundate Serbia, massive relief will be tendered and a nation of vengeful, bitter Serbs would result.

Schmitt said an Air Force inquiry theorized the F-117 stealth fighter was shot down by a SA-3 surface-to-air missile and "luck." Its radar absorbing surface, radar shattering angles and zig zag flying pattern makes it barely visible to radar at low altitude especially when opening bomb bay doors. The explanation is still under investigation.

As the author read the entire column, he wondered why the Air Force would imprudently release and publicize vital information on how the Nighthawk could be tracked, its location determined and the odds of the enemy shooting it down increased.

Rankin and Montgomery scribed that the U. S. was sending 82 more aircraft to Clinton's War on Yugoslavia. Among the composition were 24 F-16s armed with Harm anti-radar missiles, 4 A-10 Thunderbolt tank blasters, 6 EA-6B Prowler radar-jammers, 39 K-135, 2 KC-10 refueling tankers and 2 C-130 transports.

U. S. military reserves may be called up as well since "military concerned" Clinton's annual depletion of defense budgets had skeletonized the regular Air Force.

Representative Heather Wilson demanded to know what "vital national interests existed?" Of the 11-member congressional delegation that toured NATO, nine urged Clinton to prepare for a ground war!

NATO spokesman Shea said that damage to Serbia's war machine was considerable. The central direction of its air defense system was "blinded," half of its MIG "air force" eliminated, 50 percent of their fuel stocks destroyed and two of three Army Headquarters sites decimated.

Madeline's Morass and Criticisms

Pentagon officials had warned all along that air strikes wouldn't guarantee a victory. Some officials had labeled the conflict "Madeline Albright's War" wrote McManus. Mouthy, meddling, militant Madeline or M⁴ Albright retorted haughtily that the Defense Department had agreed with Clinton to launch air strikes.

Clinton and Albright assumed that a degree of action for Kosovo could be achieved by negotiations, which of course never happened. Other accomplished diplomats worried that the administration missed several opportunities to avert the war.

Albright thought a policy of diplomacy and threats of war could stop deep-seated conflicts. Others called that policy "instant insanity and wishful thinking." The idea that "representational" bombing and air strikes, predominantly U.S. with token contributions from other nations, would cause Milosevic to capitulate within a week was totally unrealistic given Yugoslavia's history of resistance to outside "imperialistic invasion."

NATO's planned celebration of its 50th anniversary and expanded age with its "newly found internal nation meddling role and declared values" statement was overshadowed by its "credibility on the line" in Serbia. Albright touted NATO's commitment to "shared interests and values" designed to ensure stability, freedom and peace for the "entire 'trans-Atlantic' area." (This policy statement is one more overt nexus to "entangle and bind the U. S. with Europe into a Western, mini one-world hegemony.")

Garhoff saw a drastic change from NATO's "defense" role to protect member nations from assault to an arrogant, enforced nation meddling "offense" role under the guise of peace and other euphemistic rationalizations that threatened its "interests and values." NATO couldn't get the UN Security Council's permission to invade Yugoslavia (because of likely

Russian and Chinese vetoes) so it ignored that route completely in order to meddle in Serbia, not defend its original mission. Such sovereign nation meddling in Europe makes a mockery that Russia has nothing to fear from NATO!

NATO "imposed" its settlement on Serbia to redefine its "hegemony" and allow Kosovo's autonomy, but not independence under the threat of bombing. It was a clear example of "diplomacy under the barrel of the gun." (It was reminiscent of Mao Tse Tung's communist policy, "diplomacy through the barrel of a gun.)

The bombings decreased Serbia's military effectiveness, minimized civilian casualties, enhanced refugee displacement, destroyed infrastructure, caused no loss of airmen's lives and still failed to bring Milosevic down. Serbs had rallied around him and were anti-NATO. Macedonia was threatened with destabilization and Germany, Italy and Greece were skeptical of NATO's intentions. New NATO members reminded all that they joined NATO for "mutual defense" and not to meddle in the internal affairs of other nations.

Parker wrote that arrogant, presumptuous Albright would "allow Serbs access to their holy places if Kosovo was 'partitioned' from Serbia."

Albright said that the NATO alliance was "wedge proof"
Despite Milosevic's charges it had cracks bound to go "poof"
    The French desired a UN arrangement,
    Russia a political denouement,
While Italy and Greece were getting queezy—"not quite aloof"

Whitney penned that aerial photos revealed "possible" mass graves of Albanians over Pristo Selo. Two parallel lines of fresh mounds were observed. Some persons speculated that military vehicles could have possibly made the lines.

Shea, NATO spokesman, said the aerial photos indicated something akin to mass graves was identified in Bosnia. No verifiable proof existed at the time.

Russia was opposed to the presence of international forces in Kosovo without Milosevic's approval as part of a diplomatic effort proffered by Albright and Gore wrote Perlez. An agreement was reached on a "verifiable end, withdrawal of military police and paramilitary forces."

Milosevic refused to sign the Rambouillet peace agreement because he wouldn't allow an international force within Serbia's sovereign borders. Albright tried to mollify Russia's objection by saying that a "NATO Core Force" would escort refugees back to Kosovo. Decision to Widen the War and Reactions

Myers related that General Clark had requested 300 more warplanes for Clinton's War on Serbia thus deepening our military involvement. Due to depletion of our regular defense personnel, U. S. Air Force reservists would be called to man and service the aircraft. F-115s and A-10s, combat support planes and refueling tankers were included in the mix.

Not 2,000 as originally publicized, but 4,800 Army troops would accompany the 24 Apaches being sent to Albania, a poor country with a dismal infrastructure.

Britain planned to send 2,000 to 3,000 troops, 20 tanks, and 50 armored personnel carriers to Macedonia in the new build up.

NATO's commanders were frustrated at the depth of Serbia's resistance. Then wanted both combat and support planes to focus on Yugoslavia's army and special police forces on a 24-hour basis.

Defense Secretary Cohen "crowed" at NATO's "tactical maneuverability" over Yugoslavia that allowed its planes to fly everywhere at will with acceptable risk, i.e., against a mere handful of MIGs and minimal, often hidden air defenses.

General Clark, however, said that Yugoslavia remained a potent enemy with "many, many targets still to be hit." It was hoped the additional planes would have a "psychological effect" on the Serbs and quickly lead to a diplomatic solution.

Enda and Schlacter wrote that General Clark was sobered by "Milosevic's willingness to accept damage," which meant a lengthened war. Meanwhile, Serbia's military capability was diminishing. One-half of his meager number of MIGs had been destroyed. Clinton ordered NATO to step up the air attacks. In addition, one British and one French aircraft carrier were expected to join the American naval task force.

At the time, Clinton was leery of dropping food, medicines and other supplies to refugees for fear the Serbs would confiscate them.

Since the cost of Clinton's War was estimated between $3 billion and $4 billion, he might submit an emergency budget to defray his induced Serbian meddling expenses. Both Clinton and British P. M. Blair were fearful that a "considerable loss of life" could occur if ground troops entered hostilities, although Clinton had not yet completely ruled out that possibility.

Senator McCain commented that adding 300 aircraft was a sign that "all was not going well in Clinton's War on Serbia."

Citizen Wasserman wrote that draft dodger Clinton now had a war of his very own. He wanted to know how Clinton decided which "ethnic cleansing" country, whites in the Balkans or blacks in Africa, was chosen. Clinton seemed to be saying; "black genocide in Africa didn't count for much." Wasserman added, "January 20, 2001 can't come too soon."

Another citizen, McMullen viewed the Serbs as "good guys" fighting to recover their birthplace of Serbian civilization in Kosovo. They were "over-whelmed and replaced by Albanian immigrants."

Serbs fight because Clinton gave them only two choices: "secure Kosovo very quickly before the bombing degrades the Serbian military" or "lose Kosovo forever." According to McMullen, Clinton, in effect, was "destroying a Christian nation on behalf of a Muslim nation."

McMullen's suggested "solution" to Clinton's War was to re-settle the Kosvars in the U. S. instead of fighting an unnecessary war. (On the contrary, a better solution might have been to re-settle Albanians in Muslim nations and avoid the unnecessary bilingual problem in education, social upheavals and unending taxpayer expenses.)

Citizen Marianadin viewed Kosovo's problem akin to Hispanics "overwhelming and replacing" whites in Southern California. NATO would blame the U. S. for not granting "autonomy and independence" to the Hispanic invaders (including millions of illegal lawbreakers). Soon thereafter, Russian led NATO forces would bomb southern California. That scenario was precisely what occurred in Kosovo.

Several questions could easily be posed, "Is the possibility so far fetched and ridiculous?" Next, "Would NATO blame the Hispanics for the exodus of "white refugees" fleeing into other states causing further "ethnic imbalances?" And, "Would continuance of that "open border" progression effectively destroy the sovereignty of the U. S.?"

Russia's Minister, Ivanov, would not agree to a KFOR in Kosovo without Milosevic's approval reported Perlez. A White House official said that a diplomatic solution to Clinton's War was not yet possible since "Milosevic hadn't yet been hurt enough by the bombing." Russian troops would probably contribute forces to the KFOR but retain their control and report directly to NATO.

Fifteen European Union countries proposed a permanent peace plan. It stipulated "Kosovo would be placed under temporary European administration if Milosevic withdrew his forces and allowed the Albanian refugees to return." NATO promised to continue bombing unless the proposal was accepted.

Germany's Chancellor Schroeder said the goal of the 15 European nations was "not to tolerate the killings and deportations in Kosovo." At the same time, he "approved military measures (more bombings) as both necessary and justified."

Gordon's column related how an F-16 had mistakenly bombed a "civilian" vehicle and caused 64 deaths and an unknown number of casualties. NATO and the Pentagon acknowledged the attack, but said they had not targeted civilians.

At first, General Clark asserted there was evidence the Serbs had shot the refugees but later retracted that assertion. Pentagon's Bacon said they "now knew" there were no signs of evidence to support Clark's comment.

Meanwhile Serb used films of the convoy carnage to inflame its people, while NATO's propaganda machine featured columns of refugees, especially women and children, fleeing the bombing to make its case.

NATO admitted that an F-16 pilot unfortunately and mistakenly bombed a civilian vehicle as an "accident of war." The pilot thought it was a military truck. NATO meekly defended itself by saying that it was unrealistic to exclude civilian casualties from intense bombardment.

According to Myers, the Pentagon sought to call up 30,000 reservists and National Guard members in a "widening the war" scenario. A "call up" would affect families, jobs, college education and employees—especially those in the aircraft industry. Air crews, pilots and support personnel would be most affected.

Clinton said only a Serb transition to democracy, not a tyrant led nation, would stabilize the Balkans. He said, "There is a solution that advances our interests and values if we are ready to make a long term commitment." Then Clinton immediately requested $5.9 billion from Congress to "widen the war."

General Shelton conceded that military success might not meet NATO's goal of returning Albanian refugees to Kosovo. In several less-than-brilliant commentaries, Defense Secretary Cohen said, "American casualties were no longer possible but probable" and "This is not going to be quick and easy or neat."

Citizen Hall viewed our involvement in Kosovo akin to our "civil war." Serbia tried to preserve its integrity as a nation by preventing Kosovo from seceding by quelling the rebel Kosovo Liberation Army.

Citizen Hall viewed the U. S. led bombings as a "war"
Not "undeclared conflict, civil war" sham we all "abhor"
    The U. S. was the big "bully" nation,

"Giant against midget" devastation,
So we "air strike" to stop the killing of each "Kosovar"

Hall hoped and prayed our leaders would find the wisdom and sagacity
Refrain from the muddled, specious course maintained with false veracity
　　Like ego, face-saving and false pride,
　　And "excuses" behind which to hide,
And find "better reasons" to justify "Slick's" bombing atrocity,

Another citizen, Lampton, asked, "How many of America's sons and daughters are going to die—just to cover up the Chinese espionage?"

Another citizen, Pollack thought it strange, except for Turkey that other Islamic countries were strangely silent about the bombings exterminating their ethnic brothers. They were quick to condemn the U. S. when suspected Muslim terrorists were bombed in Sudan and Afghanistan. Pollack asked, "Where is the Islamic support now for the Albanian Muslims?"

Citizen Base ominously predicted increased difficulty and horrible fighting. The "new McNamaras" were forecasting imminent victory and large numbers of body bags returned to America and Europe. Soon thereafter, ugly demonstrations would occur in the U. S., Canada and globally with complete discredit heaped upon Clinton, NATO and other "crisis-declared" war mongers.

Base painted a scenario where the conflict would unite Southern Slavs with Northern Slavs. Russia would lead Lithuania, Poland, Slovakia, Czech Republic and Bulgaria in defense of Serbia. Russia and China would also strangely unite as well. (Fortunately, Base's predictions proved to be erroneous.)

A Yugoslavian officer captured by Albanian insurgents was turned over to the U. S. and flown to Tirana, Italy reported Donnelly and Schlacter. Meanwhile, thousands of refugees fled toward Macedonia and Albania as NATO's bombardment continued. Yugoslavia claimed over 500 civilians had been killed and 4,000 wounded by the bombings.

The effect of "ethnic cleansing" in Kosovo created impossible logistical instabilities in Macedonia, Montenegro and Albania. It also converted Macedonia into a base for the KLA to launch attacks against Serbia.

In a speech given in Detroit, Clinton tried to justify U. S. intervention in Kosovo by posing the hypothetical question, "What if we didn't lift a finger?"

Albania's Imperialistic Dreams

Columnist Layne rejected the simplistic solution to Kosovo, which viewed Serbs as bad, Albanians as oppressed and a peace imposed on centuries old foes where both live happily ever after. On the contrary, Layne perceived the "neo-Maoist KLA fight for justice as but part of the unattainable ancient dream of a greater Albania." The dream would absorb Albania, Kosovo, parts of Montenegro, northern Greece and Macedonia through the "open border" flooding of Albanians. Such a dream could lead to new wars or alliances in an already troubled area.

Layne clearly saw a renewed "hardening of the heart" by Albanians toward Serbians. The new world order version, U. S. and Western Europe, would now have legitimate reasons galore to interfere in the international affairs of Balkan nations. The U. S.—European "one world ideologues" were mercilessly crushing nationalism wherever nations dared to raise their patriotic pennants. Remember that Turkey and Greece barely avoided war over the island of Cyprus. Perhaps the stage was being constructed to bring Montenegro, Macedonia, Albania and Romania into the "Western New World Order,"

Rubin recapped a bit of history that contended "religious identity bound with nationality" were important reasons for antagonisms that existed among Muslims, Orthodox Christians and Western Christians. The antagonisms had raged for centuries and each faith had sought hegemony over the region at various times.

Serbs viewed NATO's war as a conflict between Eastern and Western Christianity. Gage, Greek Orthodox writer, perceived NATO's bombing as "misguided" policy that was going to bring tragedy to a lot of people."

The Serbs considered Kosovo as "Serbian Jerusalm where its earliest Serbian Orthodox churches and monasteries are located. Kosovo "must' remain part of Serbia. On the other hand, some Albanians in Kosovo felt that "de facto" ownership of land in the province" gives them the right to appropriate by "open border inundation," land legally part of Serbia, now a part of the larger Albanian State.

(This situation is a prelude of peril that results from the global policy of "open borders, denationalization and desovereignization." It provides a precedent for imperialistic meddling in the internal affairs of other nations by "international forces a la NATO, United Nations et al." Its credo and objectives are to "neutralize and/or stamp out nationalism" or "we'll bomb the hell out of you and bury you under the euphemism of our 'peaceful' intentions." Nationalism, as a concept and powerful, people unifying, patriotic entity would be "strategically preserved" as a deranged illusion in name only—in a practical one world government hegemony!

Chapter 4

Intensification of the War, Refugee Plan and Prelude and Release of U. S. POWs

Clinton's War intensified because the "instant end to the war strategy" he envisioned had failed and Milosevic was not yet ready to capitulate and come to the peace table. This chapter chronologically describes events under the headings of Further Intensification of Clinton's War and Reactions, Clinton's Plan to Accept Albanian Refugees, NATO's "New" War and Reactions, House Tie Vote Fails to Support Use of Ground Troops or Air Strikes, Prelude to and Release of Three U. S. POWs and Arrival of First Group of Refugees to America. Other news releases are interspersed among the main headings.

Further Intensification of Clinton's War and Reactions

With complete characteristic absence of candor, conniving Clinton said, "Ground troops would not be ruled out in the absence of a permissive environment." In other words, Clinton's War could involve ground troops whether Serbia extended an invitation or not. At the same time Clinton was introducing Apache helicopters, Warthog war planes, enlarged naval task forces and U. S. led NATO troops holed up in Macedonia as a military bluff and/or preparation for a land war.

The column by Thomma and Schlacter described how Serbian troops forced Albanians to dig most graves for their deceased. Italian General Marani disclosed that 43 burial sites were identified as part of an estimated 3,200 Albanians killed. The graves appeared to be individual plots, pointed to the Southwest toward the holy city of Mecca in Saudi Arabia as a "bow to Muslim practice."

After 26 days of aggression, Yugoslav Foreign Minister Jovanovic said, "Be sure that we can resist any kind of attacks, any kind of aggression."

In the meantime, NATO was busy shutting down all petroleum sources within Serbia by bombing its refineries and distribution networks. The pipeline for Croatia was closed and the U. S. was urging other countries not to ship petroleum to Yugoslavia.

One world advocate ideologue, Department of State Strobe Talbot, denied NATO was losing the war against a nation the size of Ohio and expressed confidence that "air power alone would do the job." He was not in favor or arming the KLA to fight for its people. Talbot had no desire to militarize or involve locals (Albanians). Instead, the "utopian" objective was to "demilitarize the situation so Serbians and Albanians could put aside their ancient religious and cultural hatreds and live in peace."

As per Schmitt and Myers, the columnists noted that certain NATO targets had become "personalized" and designated for air strikes. The targets were businesses owned by political friends of Milosevic. Among the targets included were Yugo Petrol and Dragan Tomic its director (speaker of parliament in Belgrade), Zastava auto plant and Milan Beko its director (former minister of privatization) of tobacco factory and warehouse and Marko Milosevic (son of Milosevic) its owner and major player in tobacco distribution. Up to this point, NATO's targets had been predominantly military and only a dozen or so had been "civilian." The "architect of personal destruction" had taken over.

Obviously the bombing had thus far failed to halt "ethnic cleansing" of Albanians from Kosovo. General Clark believed that intensified bombing would decrease Milosevic's ability to wage war and eventually force him to accept peace terms.

At the same time, other NATO "political leaders" were in the process of approving Serbian sites targeted for decimation. NATO's policy seemed designed to "impose peace at all costs even if it had to bomb the Serbs into the peace of the grave!"

Breor, citizen, observed that Reagan used the might of the U. S. military to combat the "threat of communism" while Clinton used America's military power to "impose 'forced peace' around the world."

After more than 6,000 sorties, NATO's forces had failed to halt Yugoslavia's offensive in Kosovo spearheaded by 8,000 Serbian troops reported Myers.

At the same time, NATO was negotiating with leaders of Romania, Albania and Hungary to allow "over flights" from provisional bases to accommodate more than 300 more aircraft in a new "widening the war" effort. The facilities at Aviana, Italy had become overloaded. Turkey and Hungary were the selected sites for proposed new air bases. In addition, the aircraft carrier USS Enterprise was under serious consideration as an addition to the naval task force.

NATO was pleased with successful strikes against Yugoslavia's oil industry. NATO also noted the Serb's difficulty in "quashing the KLA" as it sent reinforcements to Kosovo. General Clark et al. felt frustrated by NATO's inability to halt "ethnic cleansing" of Albanians in Kosovo.

Unabashedly, Clinton appealed to Congress for $6 billion more in emergency funds for "*conducting the war because it was clearly in our national interest and lives were hanging in the balance!*"

Clinton still maintained that no plans existed to send ground troops to Kosovo according to McFeatters. Although most of the public and Congress led by Senator McCain believed otherwise, Clinton was adamant. Senator Lugar opined that "poll-driven" Clinton was "incompetent and

duplicitous" and should extricate himself from this "ill-begotten war."
Many others believed similarly. According to Senator McCain, "Clinton's
credibility had lapsed into nothingness."

(The author never for a moment believed the Pentagon didn't have a
contingency plan in place for ground troop invasion if deemed necessary;
otherwise, it would have remiss in its duty.)

After four weeks of intense bombing and failing to capitulate, Serbia
resorted to using 700 Kosovar boys as blood donors for wounded Serbian
soldiers wrote Thomma and Schlacter. In the city of Pec, captured young
Albanian women in a hotel were made "available" for intimate services to
hand picked Serbian solders.

A bipartisan group of seven senators led by Senator McCain introduced
a resolution that would allow Clinton to "use all necessary force" in pros-
ecuting the war to an early end. Such a move would grant Clinton with
the legal structure for using ground troops which he adamantly "loophole
like" opposed.

Citizen Pirone believed the War Powers Act that Congress authorized
was to allow the president to respond quickly to a nuclear attack. Clinton
abused this power by using it politically to attack Serbia. Pirone also
observed that air power alone had never won a war.

Jason recalled NATO's "inaction" in 1989 when Croatians and
Bosnians brutally "ethnically cleansed" 200,000 Serbs out of the area. He
remembered that there was no outcry from the U. S., NATO or the UN
at the time.

He viewed the KLA as a brutal guerrilla force armed by German supporters hell-bent on "ethnically cleansing" Serbs out of Kosovo, the ances-
tral religious land of Serbian Jerusalem.

Barringtron couldn't comprehend how the world's religious leaders
were strangely silent during "ethnic cleansing" in Kosovo. It reminded
him of their "mutism" when the American Indians were forced from their
native lands to government reservations and Japanese-Americans interned
in re-location camps during W. W. II.

The column by Rankin, Enda and Montgomery disclosed that up to 20 thousand Albanians would be brought to the U. S. to live with relatives and volunteers. Gore said they would remain until it was "safe to return."

(Clinton's humane plan to accept refugees was in keeping with the political-multicultural grand design to Balkanize America at every opportunity. Precedents had already been established with "refugees" invited from Russia, Israel, Mexico, Central and South America, South Korea, Vietnam, Afghanistan, Iraq, Taiwan, China and other "militarily, politically, economically and socially stressed out 'asylum seeking victim' nations."

Cohen and Albright wanted to continue air attacks but rejected ground troop use in a "hostile and non-permissive environment." A White House spokesman said the "use of troops" would be reviewed.

The British and French wanted the U. S. to seriously consider using troops. NATO officials, however, had left the issue off its agenda on the eve of its 50th year celebration of its existence.

To date, the bombings had destroyed the last bridge over the Danube, and an estimated 850,000 Albanians had fled Kosovo.

Clinton's Plan to Accept Albanian Refugees

Harden's column described a White House relocation plan to bring 20,000 Kosovar refugees to the U. S. and make them all eligible for permanent residence. The White House official said many refugees would choose not to return to Kosovo. U. S. Albanian groups were angry because it signaled that many refugees would not be able to return to Kosovo anytime soon.

Gore announced that those refugees who had families in the U. S. and were not at risk with illness would be welcome. He said unbelievably that it was not asylum; rather, "we anticipate their return to Kosovo!"

U. S. law permits 75,000 refugees from around the world to be accepted with full federal housing, health and job assistance benefits. After

12 months, they could opt to accept a green card, which bestows permanent residence status.

Some refugees had criticized transfers to third countries, saying the procedure splits up families and some didn't want to leave the region. Refugees were seen weeping as they boarded a plane for Turkey. A half-million Albanians are already in the U. S. living mostly in the New York metropolitan area.

Leavy, National Security Council, said that each refugee may refuse to come and all have their return flights paid, so they can go back. "Realistically, once you send refugees out of a region, their chances of return are small," remarked Mistafij of the New York Kosovo Relief Fund. Others criticized re-location because the message relayed is that "ethnic cleansing" was an accomplished fact.

"I feel your pain" Clinton realized that sending them to Guantanamo in "prison-like isolation" far from their families and others might not be appropriate. The move would also remove some pressure on Macedonia, which had a 2:1 ratio of Slavs to Albanians. This plan was a small part of the overall military operation to get them back to their homes.

(Clinton's relocation plan, of course, was in keeping with his often-stated arrogant intention to multiculturize and Balkanize the U. S. That intention also dovetailed with his desire to levelize the U. S. in every way possible in order to attain more easily his ultimate one world government objective, i. e., "subjugation, enslavement and denationalization of all nations.")

An anonymous Boston Globe blurb reported that international journalists denounced NATO's bombing of Serbia's State television station because it put them in peril by endangering their lives. They admitted the station was used as a propaganda transmitter; however, the attack was quite ruthless and ineffective because it was soon back on the air at the same location.

Serbian authorities claimed approximately 150 persons were in the building, 10 were killed and about 20 others were buried in the rubble.

NATO's 50th anniversary was aggressively and imperialistically "celebrated" in Washington on April 23, 1999. Alas, it was not a Serbian victory celebration. Its 19 defense ministers agreed to impose an oil embargo on Serbia by searching tankers in the Adriatic. NATO ordered General Clark to carry out air strikes against overland pipelines and railroads that transported fuel from Montenegro to Serbia.

"Bombs at the ready" diplomat Albright said that just bombing Serbia's refineries and distribution operations was insufficient; other sources of oil must be bombed as well. Care would be taken not to bomb Montenegro's internal oil storage, however.

> NATO's latest communiqué stated that the bombing would cease
> If Milosevic withdrew all troops from Kosovo in surcease
>> Permit NATO's huge military force
>> Install a provisional "gov" perforce,
> And "give" Kosovo limited autonomy for "imposed" peace

Imperialistic NATO also pledged to seek a diplomatic solution from the UN Security Council and hoped that Russia would become a partner. The intent was clear. Serbia must not stand in the way of U. S. led NATO's brand of imperialism and effective, total destruction of European nationalism. The intention of NATO echoed Albright's oft-stated promise "not to hesitate to use military force to achieve our goal."

NATO's "New" Agenda and Reactions

Clinton said that Milosevic would capitulate when he realized that NATO's bombings would prevail, degrade his military and make his policy of ethnic cleansing too costly to continue wrote Enda, Donnelly and Parker. Clinton defended NATO's first "offensive war for interdependence" in history and promised to rebuild the Balkans.

NATO's "new global agenda" expanded its policy of meddling into the internal affairs of other sovereign nations. It included "combating terrorism, halting the spread of nuclear, chemical and biological weapons and policing other internal conflicts 'beyond the borders' of its 19 member nations." Military forced hegemony over all of Western Europe was the order of the day and blatantly declared as new policy.

Eastern European nations including especially Russia and its former nation states would continue to be wooed, enticed and bribed with economic assistance and loans until they can be "peacefully" enveloped into the "U. S.—Europe, mini Western one world" organization.

As is now evident in Serbia, the relentless policy of "denationalization and a border-less Europe" would be pursued and implemented by military force with almost complete disdain for "national desires" that might impede integration. NATO's arrogant imperialists had already openly declared its readiness to meddle in any regional and ethnic conflict beyond NATO's borders.

Clinton and NATO leaders planned to re-construct the Balkans region including Serbia, Montenegro, Macedonia, Albania et al. after hostilities ceased at an estimated cost of $35 billion. Germany had already assembled a 5-year, $35 billion package to help integrate the Balkans into the European economic mainstream.

The entire Balkan region would eventually be integrated into NATO to "prevent" ethnic hostility from ever rising again! It reminded the author of perennial, political fairy tales heard in the idealistic past that "peace, prosperity, stability and shared decision making would reign and every nation would live happily ever after." The only difference from the past was that "utopia would not be 'negotiated, but militarily imposed uber alles."

France labeled NATO's plan to block tankers on the high seas as "an act of war." Russia rejected the oil embargo outright and worried it bore the seeds of a "third world war."

Agnes Scott College Political Science Professor Agnes Scott noted that America's foreign policy first bombed a sovereign state for violating human rights although propagandized as a humanitarian effort. The bombings effectively symbolized the New World Order objective as "supreme law uber alles."

Scott likened the attack on Serbia to "rescuing" Kuwait but neglected to mention the vital oil motive. She wrote of rescuing white settlers captured by savage Indians, POWs in Vietnam, hostages in Iraq and the three soldiers recently taken prisoner in Serbia.

She also recalled propaganda efforts to "demonize" enemies of the State like Milosevic (Serbia), Noriega (Panama), Saddam Hussein (Iraq) and Mohamed Farah Aidid (Somalia).

Clinton's air attack on Serbia was premised on "America's role as rescuer and doing our duty to right wrong in the world" as presumptuously promulgated by him. Unfortunately, doing what is "right" was never clearly defined. Scott cautioned that it would be advantageous to reflect and debate our role in the world before answering the important questions about duty, moral action and foreign policy.

(Scott's thought provoking column did not explicitly mention that present Serbian policy was merely one stratagem, along with trade pacts, human rights violations, environmental controls, nuclear-chemical-biological treaties and related that serve as "justifications" to meddle in the internal affairs of other sovereign nations in panting, perilous pursuit of a puissant one world government.")

Citizen Randles called for the UN to work toward a negotiated peace. He opined that NATO's bombardment caused suffering, death, destruction of the infrastructure and irreparable damage to the environment. He thought it was counterproductive to prolong air strikes or send in ground troops.

Randles was puzzled that France, Italy and Greece rejected an oil blockade of Yugoslavia because of "legalities," but were united in bombing people. He was outraged that the "value of oil was more important than blood."

Kempster and Marshall described NATO's Secretary General Solana's declaration that "**human rights violations and rights of minorities every day were more important than sovereign borders!**" On Day 32 of Clinton's War, Solana was more concerned with forced fleeing of refugees from Kosovo than with Serbia's sovereignty. He also wanted Russia to become "partner" in solving the regional crisis in the "Euro-Atlantic" area.

NATO promised to fight for Macedonia, Albania and other countries if the war transcended both borders. It also promised to help reconstruct the area after the war reported Yemma.

Meanwhile, Hungary agreed to let NATO use its air base. The last remaining bridge spanning the Danube near Novi Sad was destroyed. Counting 4,000 additional British and German troops deployed in Macedonia, NATO's forces now numbered 28,000.

Gordon scribed that NATO must make concessions to Serbia in order to end the war according to Russia's Foreign Minister Ivanov. One worlder, borderless nation proponent, Strobe Talbot, was in Moscow seeking possible Russian mediation in order to halt the air war. Ivanov, however, was not in any mood to serve as "postal carrier" to deliver NATO's ultimatum to Serbia. He said that cooperation, not ultimatums, was essential.

Ivanov revealed that Milosevic appeared ready to reduce forces to levels of October 1998 and allow an international presence in Kosovo. Other details were not revealed.

Apparently Talbot's visit to Moscow was designed to seek Moscow's active participation in ending the war on Serbia, although similar requests extended by Russia to end the war in Iraq were strangely labeled "meddlesome."

Safire's column exposed the gaff that stealth bombers were flown half way around the world to "engage in a tactical mission." He also downplayed the Apache gun ship as "the weapon of salvation," which would destroy Serbian tanks and halt the exodus of Albanians. Apaches, according to an anonymous tank expert, are vulnerable to small arms fire and even rocks. Apaches are most effective as spotters for artillery and in destroying emplacements and small units, but only as part of a coordinated ground attack. In sum, Apaches, as a panacea, they are not.

Safire wrote that "Big Lie" propaganda was in motion. It allowed NATO and Serbia to claim victory. NATO gets Serbia to withdraw its military, but not the police from Kosovo, the right of Albanians to return and war crimes trials for both Serbia's paramilitary and KLA guerrillas. Serbia retains full sovereignty over Kosovo, the right of unarmed refugees to return and presence of unarmed UN observers led by Russia.

Clinton authorized the Pentagon to activate 33,102 National Guard troops and military reservists reported Thomma and Parker. The stated purpose was to allow NATO to bomb simultaneously military targets all over Serbia as "ordered" by NATO leaders.

The first call up of reserves would be used to help refuel the additional 100 aerial tankers and other NATO aircraft. Lockhart said that Clinton was "fully cognizant that it (the call up of reserves) disrupted lives."

House Tie Vote Fails to Support Use of Ground Troops or Air Strikes

The House voted 240—180 to require Clinton to seek congressional approval before using ground troops in Serbia related Mitchell. Another House vote was 213 to 213 that failed to give symbolic support to Clinton's air bombardment of Serbia. Both votes suggested deep division among House legislators regarding the Serbian War. Some House members preferred to withdraw from the Balkans.

Hastert interpreted the votes as signs that Clinton should "better explain the goals, costs and the long-term objective of why we're here."

The arrogant White House, as expected, said it didn't need the "moral support" of the House to continue air bombardment decimation of Serbia. Candid Clinton "vowed" to seek congressional support if he decided to use ground troops.

Senator McCain introduced a resolution to authorize Clinton to "use all necessary force to win." Senator Lott immediately objected to the resolution.

Representative Rogan didn't want to "jeopardize our military strength by injecting ourselves into every civil conflict in the world."

Erlanger's column highlighted the fact that NATO's air attacks have created unemployment for thousands in Yugoslavia. Destruction of auto-truck and munitions factories displaced 15,000 workers, the Soboda Works at Cakak dislocated 5,000 employees and the Okobar plant at Kruseva left 7,000 people out of work.

Oil refineries and most storage tanks were also put out of commission by air bombardment. Serbia's economic output has been virtually halted with over an estimated 100,000 persons becoming unemployed.

NATO was now bombing "high value targets" dear to Milosevic and friends. They were actually civilian targets that included government buildings and cigarette and fertilizer factories. Chemical factories that emit toxic fumes and cause widespread environmental damage were prime targets, too. Overall, Serbia's industrial base was being systematically destroyed.

After hostilities ceased, re-building costs were estimated at between $40 billion to $100 billion. The overall cost of Clinton's War was not disclosed in the column.

Hess commented that failure by the House to back Clinton's air war kindled a partisan uproar. Hastert asserted that the House vote sent a message to Clinton that he must fully explain his rationale to the American people and Congress for U. S. involvement in Serbia.

Clinton appointee, Defense Secretary Cohen, contended that the House vote "conflicts with the 'strong' solidarity of the NATO leaders; it was 'counterproductive.'"

Naturally Democrats blamed "right wing extremist Republicans." Bonior noted the hypocrisy and said, "Ninety-two Republicans voted against withdrawal of our troops but only 31 voted to support the air campaign."

Armey criticized Clinton for "going forward, after the fact, consults with us after the fact, and then, frankly, wants us to give them a validation." They warned Democrats the House vote would be "iffy" and not worth the risk of failure.

NATO's incessant murderous bombing had galvanized and invigorated the Serbian Army personnel penned Harden and Myers. They were rallying to the defense of their country, more recruits were heeding the draft and enlisting and the rallying point was NATO, the enemy.

Some observers said the Yugosolavian Army in Kosovo was intact and remained so by dispersing its forces to minimize casualties from bombardment. General Clark acknowledged that assessment. The Yugoslav Army was then perceived as the defender of the nation.

Prelude to and Release of Three U. S. Prisoners

Serbs allowed Jesse Jackson to speak to the three POWs in Belgrade's Military Court Building on April 30, 1999 as per Sach's column. Exhibiting evident emotion, the young POWs were allowed to send messages home. The visit lasted 40 minutes.

Political opportunist, Representative Blagojevich, member of the House Armed Services Committee, declared that he'd make sure the captives received a pay raise—for being captured!

Details of the health and condition of the captives were not released by the Yugoslavian government at the time; however, the three POWs appeared to look fit, though tired and mentally drained. They wore boots without laces.

> The three POWs appeared most anxious, nervous and tense
> Evidenced extreme tension with hopeful "release suspense"
>> Seated ramrod straight on their chairs,
>> Expression-less—with vacant stares,
> Dressed in Army camouflage and lace-less boots sans pretense

Stone looked very tired with dark worry circles under his eyes
The forehead bruise was clearly evident, not "pan caked" in disguise
    Gonzalez was somewhat mentally drained,
    But okay overall, though clearly strained,
And Ramirez was grateful for "His" prayers on which he relies

An anonymous Associated Press release recalled that Jesse Jackson had a history of acting as "unofficial diplomat" in international crises. He lobbied for Mid East peace in 1979 and arranged for Navy Lieutenant Goodman's release after being shot down by Syrian antiaircraft guns in Lebanon in 1984. In 1990, Jackson secured the release of a dozen American hostages from Iraq, acted to inform Haitian military leaders that an invasion was imminent in 1993 and delivered a message to Nigeria from Clinton for the lack of progress in restoring democracy in 1994.

Milosevic freed the three American POWs to Jesse Jackson on May 1, 1999 as a step toward ending 39 days of air strikes wrote Boudreaux and Williams. Lieutenant General Kovasevic signed their release to Jackson's delegation of religious leaders. Dr. Nazir Uddin Khaja, American Muslim Council and Rabbi Steven Bennett Jacobs, both from Los Angeles accompanied Jackson, although Clinton had discouraged their journey.

Milosevic decided on the release after a three-hour parley with his advisors and Jackson. No conditions on the release of the POWs were set and Jackson was given a letter to Clinton requesting a face-to-face meeting.

Jesse crossed the room to gather the three POWs in embrace
Thanked the Almighty Father for His kind, loving "mercy and grace"
    Turned over his handy, personal cell phone,
    So three POWs could eagerly call home,
Then preached, "Let nations not rise up against nations" for war's "erase"

As the soldiers telephoned home, the event became a "tearfest"
Even Jesse was teary eyed as he prevailed in this "weepfest"

> The POWs traveled to Ramstein Air Base
> In Germany for medical tests, solace
> And debriefing that provided "info," closure and needed rest

Jackson urged both sides to step up diplomatic efforts to end the conflict, halt the bombing and give Yugoslavia a "night of peace from bombs." NATO promptly dismissed Jesse's request and immediately issued orders to "step up the air attacks."

An anonymous Associated Press blurb disclosed that, on successive days, an F-16 crashed in Western Serbia and an AV-8B Harrier plunged into the Adriatic Sea. Fortunately, pilots of both planes were rescued in good physical health.

NATO also acknowledged a deadly missile attack on a civilian bus with unknown casualties. NATO's Shea said there would be no respite from air strikes even though the three American POWs had been released.

Sacks wrote how one POW found comfort from drawing an American flag on toilet tissue and two other prisoners sought solace in prayer. They were kept in virtual isolation for 31 days.

During the flight from Belgrade to Germany, the POWs were extremely hungry and wolfed down pizzas and hamburgers. Jesse Jackson and his inter-faith delegation accompanied the POWs to Ramstein Air Base.

Doctors at Ramstein Air Base, Germany examined the trio of POWs and pronounced them in "apparent" good health. A 48—72 hour medical and psychological testing period was scheduled along with military debriefing.

Jackson said release of the POWs was an opportunity to "break the cycle of violence" and "Clinton must weigh in" on the situation. Others said that Milosevic released the POWs as a cynical gesture.

At the time of their release, they had mixed emotions. When first taken as prisoners, they were kicked and beaten and had hoods placed over their heads. Later, the guards were very kind. The three POWs shook hands with the guards and would continue to pray for an end to the crisis.

Clinton and Russian envoy, Chernomyrdin, met to discuss possible solutions to Clinton's War scribed Perlez. He agreed to see the envoy at Yeltsin's request, although the air strikes would continue.

Strobe Talbot dismissed the letter from Milosevic to Clinton requesting a vis-à-vis meeting as simply a "PR stunt." NATO's spokesman Shea remarked that Milosevic should not expect a "reward" for releasing the three POWs.

As per a previously scheduled itinerary, Clinton planned to visit NATO Headquarters and the troops based in Germany, then on to London and Paris. The "photo op" visits by the top banana would attempt to counter Jesse Jackson's "good will" release of the POWs and blunt Chernomyrdin's planned "shuttle diplomacy" trip in the interest of peace with UN's Annan in New York.

Wendland described the joy of the three POWs and their families as they were reunited. They touched, hugged, kissed and embraced each other with fervor. It was an euphoric occasion.

Major General Grange commented that the POWs would undergo a three-day briefing to learn what might be useful for training purposes. He noted they looked better than when first captured. The POWs related they were fed lots of soup and bread while in captivity and lost some weight as a result.

Ramirez had two fractured ribs, a one and one-half inch cut on his head and a swollen right leg. Stone's face had cuts and bruises on his face plus a broken nose.

Russian envoy Chernomyrdin and Jesse Jackson delivered several pleas for peace to Clinton, but to no avail wrote Thomma and Donnelly. Chernomyrdin told Clinton that Milosevic was in a "negotiating" mood. Jackson asked Clinton to telephone Milosevic to let two Serbian POWs held in Germany go free as a good will gesture.

Generalissimo Clinton appreciated the return of the three POWs and reiterated his vow to continue murderous, devastating air bombardment "until the million-plus Albanian refugees returned to their Kosovo residences." It was essentially an empty gesture because of the fact that most "residences" had been bombed or burned into "non-existence."

Gordon reported that NATO's military-civilian bombardment had cut off 70 percent of Yugoslavia's electric power meant to disrupt communications, command centers and air defense systems. Electrical disruption was caused by the use of special bombs that contained strands of carbon that "short circuited" transformers but did not destroy them.

NATO insisted that power to hospitals and other vital civilian services would not be cut since "they had back up generators fueled by diesel oil!"

Critics warned that repeated attacks on electric power plants could force closure of facilities for water purification and sewage treatment, damage hospital operation and undermine public support for NATO's strategy.

Citizen Baker observed that Clinton's foreign policy was "incompetent and a complete failure." He noted that Americans were obsessed with the 13 children killed at Littleton, Colorado but were relatively unconcerned about the vast numbers of Serbian and Albanian children killed in Yugoslavia. He wondered if the loss of Yugoslavian children meant less to those parents than deaths of children to parents living in Littleton.

Baker also opined that Clinton was "hardened" against Jesse Jackson's peace suggestion.

Citizen Jensen echoed Baker's sentiments in re Clinton's rebuff of Jackson's plea for peace negotiation. He thought of the carnage on a bus bombed by "NATO" macho pilots and wondered if they wanted to be associated with this grisly event.

Another citizen, Laurie, was keenly aware that bombing would accomplish NATO's objectives. He said that NATO was systematically destroying Serbia's industries, infrastructure and resources. He wondered if journalist's news footage would be balanced with pictures showing that Serbia's young, elderly and weak were dying and food, fuel and medicine were scarce and running out akin to pictures they readily displayed of Albanian refugees.

An anonymous Associated Press blurb revealed that Clinton was considering the release of two captured Serb POWs a few days after Jesse Jackson suggested quick action as a gesture of good will.

A short anonymous Knight-Ridder news item said the Congress was perplexed on how to deal with Clinton's War. Six weeks ago, the Senate voted to support the air war. Last week, the House voted "not to use all necessary force to prosecute the war."

Some critics said that Clinton had "neither the moral courage nor the competence to run the war." Senator McCain didn't believe that "Clinton was prepared to lose the war where 'our interests and values were imperiled.'"

Safire thought that NATO's unwillingness to invade Kosovo at the beginning of the war was a prescription for defeat. It hoped that air strikes would force Milosevic, with Russian assistance, to negotiate and surrender all he had won on the battlefield. Clinton was using all necessary force to establish the principle that "no nation can drive out an unwanted people."

Safire downplayed the notions of intervention versus isolation, uncontrolled versus controlled national borders and imposed versus self-determination, which in fact were the central issues. He did not trust Clinton to use all force necessary to establish the principle that "no nation can drive out an unwanted people."

(As stated previously, "Clinton's central imperialistic motive 'was and is' to pursue and expand NATO's authority to establish a mini, one-world U. S.—Western Europe hegemony to meddle into the internal affairs of any nation for any reason including the 'threat to peace.'" In the process, the U. S. would be "legally" bound to engage in hostilities anywhere in Western Europe. War time participation would be "sold and propagandized" under the banners of "world peace, national interest, national security, superpower responsibility, moral requirement and related propagandist, horse hockey euphemisms.")

Arrival of the First Group of Refugees to America

Four hundred and fifty-three refugees (453) arrived at McQuire Air Force Base from Macedonia, the first of 20 thousand. They would be located at Fort Dix where they will be housed, medicated and fed. All precautions for their safety had been taken.

Ever "photo op" conscious Hillary was on hand to greet the refugees. She welcomed them and promised, "We will not let Mr. Milosevic succeed in keeping you out of your homes." She even mouthed "Mursevi ne Amerike" or "welcome to America."

The INS fingerprinted them and issued I Ds, sweat suits and toiletries. The White House scrapped initial plans to restrict refugees arriving that allowed them to stay with relatives willing to sponsor them. Instead, nine non-profit relief agencies would sponsor refugees and find them apartments. Islamic Relief said that 25 families in Burbank, California would welcome refugees into their homes.

Host families would assist refugees to apply for social security, welfare and money for transportation according to Huffaker's column.

The first baby, a boy, was born to a Kosovo refugee less than 24 hours after his mother, Lebibe, arrived in America. The parents were Mr. and Mrs. Naim Karaliju.

A joint statement on ending Clinton's War was expected wrote Cohen. An international civil and security presence, not labeled NATO but under UN mandate, after withdrawal of Serbian forces from Kosovo and an unrealistic return of all refugees, were expected to be in the agreement. It was designed to increase Milosevic's isolation, i. e., with Russia's participation.

Clinton, meanwhile, made a two-day crisis visit to "cement allied unity over U. S. led pulverization of Yugoslavia." Naturally, he wanted to embrace Russia and other Slavic states to join in the "solidarity mission."

"Draft dodger" Clinton, never one to miss a "positive" photo op with the military, posed with the three recently released POWs. He was shamelessly attired in a U. S. A. F. bomber jacket as evidenced by a photo taken by Walsh, Associated Press.

Seelye's described Clinton's two-day peace crisis excursion to Brussels that included visits with the Group of Seven, NATO commanders, Germany's Chancellor Schroeder, relief agency officials handling the refugee crisis and personnel at two air bases.

At Spangdahlem, Clinton addressed the troops and stated that he was extremely proud of them. He assured them of congressional bipartisan support for a pay raise.

Russia finally agreed that an international and civilian force was necessary to keep eventual peace in Kosovo wrote Cohen. Differences still existed between Russia and the Group of Seven including withdrawal of "all" Serbian forces from Kosovo, agreement by Milosevic for presence of NATO forces in Kosovo, demilitarization of the KLA, self government for Kosovo and return of refugees—all contentious issues.

Russia still objected to any "imposed" solution and believed the only possible solution lay in an agreement with Milosevic.

Enda's column described Clinton's meetings with 334 refugee families in Ingelheim, Germany. Clinton said that "ethnic cleansing must be opposed, resisted and reversed." It was Clinton's first meeting with the people he promised to protect by ordering air strikes.

Chapter 5

Bombing the Chinese Embassy, NIMA, White House Pique With Release of POWs and Peace Negotiations

This chapter describes Chinese Embassy Bombing, Protestations and other Reactions; National Imagery and Mapping Agency, NIMA, and Inaccurate Civilian-Military Maps; Jesse Jackson's Release of the POWs and White House Consternation, Ongoing Peace Negotiations—Beginning of the Thaw, Los Angeles Fetes the POWs as Heroes, Bombing Beat Goes On—Air Strikes Continue Mercilessly and Milosevic and Four Aides Indicted as War Criminals and Peace Feelers. Other pertinent news events are chronologically interspersed among the main headings.

Chines Embassy Bombing, Protestations and other Reactions

Myers' column described NATO's "mistaken or ineffective intelligence" bombing of the Chinese Embassy in Belgrade. China's ambassador to the UN, Qin Huasun, called "NATO's barbarian act a violation of the UN Charter." Two Chinese citizens were killed and two others reported missing.

China called on NATO to halt the bombings that had already caused "great civilian casualties." Huasun wanted to avoid "further humanitarian disasters." NATO, however, was undismayed by China's concerns and continued the massive air strikes.

Last week, NATO bombed a hospital complex and marketplace at Nix where 15 Yugloslavs were killed and 60 to 70 civilians reported wounded.

USAF Major General Wald admitted that laser-guided bombs were only 80 to 90 percent accurate according to Richter. The "surgical" air strike strategy was killing too many civilians in the hospital, marketplace and Chinese Embassy. Defensive proponents of the air strikes euphemistically termed the civilian victims of bombing as "collateral damage."

The Chinese Embassy, "collaterally damaged" by an F-117, resulted in the deaths of three Chinese and 20 civilians wounded. NATO erroneously thought the Chinese Embassy was a "munitions storage depot!" Apparently NATO "experts" failed to double-check their information and maps before the bombing was ordered. Seven major "incidents" had already occurred in which NATO admitted its aircraft had "accidentally" bombed civilian targets. Either or both, "intelligence and delivery," had been faulty.

NATO's air bombardment had targeted seven civilian "sites" by mistake
Included a convoy of innocent Albanian Muslims crushed in its wake
    Passengers riding a bus and a train,
    Victims in hospital with severe pain,
Shoppers and Chinese Embassy workers that revealed "less than precise bombing" quake

Although the Chinese Embassy was in operation for two years, NATO's intelligence thought it was a "munitions storage facility" as per Rubin, Marshall and Boudreaux. NATO blamed "faulty intelligence" and apologized with deep regret. UN Secretary General Solana was "visibly upset." Clinton said, "It was a tragic mistake." U. S. Ambassador Sasser delivered a formal apology to China.

China and Russia vigorously protested the attack. Thousands of Chinese students marched on the U. S. Embassy in Beijing. Placards showed the Nazi swastika linked to NATO with phrases like "USA go to Hell," and "Down with U. S. Imperialism."

Russian envoy Chernomyrdin called the attack "barbarian." Foreign Minister Ivanov labeled the attack "unconscionable and direct provocation."

Tens of thousands of Chinese demonstrated at the U. S. Consulate compound in Chengdu, broke into it and severely burned the consulate's residence wrote Schoof. Other U. S. buildings across China were protested against as well. The protesters shouted, "Severely punish the killers," "Break up NATO" and other slogans.

The U. S. Embassy in Beijing had more than 10,000 protesters, who threw rocks, burned newspapers and threw paving stones and paint freely about. Even the U. S. Embassy emblem was torn off its gate.

U. S. Ambassador Sasser felt they were under siege without adequate security. He and other officials advised Americans in the area to "raise their security awareness."

As he looked over tornado damage in Oklahoma, Clinton took time to apologize to the Chinese for bombing its embassy in Belgrade reported Knight-Ridder. He wanted the Chinese to "recall that the reason for the bombing was to stop the slaughter of Albanian Muslims and their exodus from Kosovo by Serbian Christians!"

Boris Yeltsin called the bombing a "barbarous and inhuman act"
Then ordered a peace trip to Britain by Ivanov canceled in fact
    UN's Solana profusely apologized,
    To China's ambassador as he agonized
That "unconditional peace" was set back by this "misguided attack"

China viewed the attack on its embassy in Belgrade as "deliberate" for its opposition to air strikes over Kosovo wrote Chu and Farley. U. S. Consulates at Shanghai, Hong Kong and Guangzhou were recipients of anti-American protest rallies. Even the U. S. Consulate's residence in Chengdu was burned. As a consequence, U. S.—Chinese relations had become more restrained and contentious with disputes over human rights, trade and alleged Chinese espionage.

College students had burned U. S. flags, shouted slogans, burned U. S. dollars, sang China's national anthem and pelted rocks at the U. S. Embassy and its vehicles in Beijing. Similar protests occurred in Shanghai and Chengdu. One Chinese protester accurately accused the U. S. of "acting as an arrogant superpower bent on globally imposing its police power according to its own interests."

China's reaction to the bombing of its embassy resulted in severance of diplomatic talks on "human rights and arms control" wrote Schoof. Clinton then responded by suspending talks on "weapons proliferation and international security" according to Zhu Banjzao.

China's Ambassador to the U. S., Li Zhaoxing, announced that China would not accept American propaganda attempts to "whitewash the atrocity as a mistake."

Many Chinese in Beijing protested the attack on its embassy in Belgrade. Some placards had messages like "A debt of blood must be repaid in blood, "Down with the U. S." and "Protect the fatherland's sovereignty."

The Chinese ambassador to the U. S., Li Zaoxing
Stated that China would not accept the "whitewash, mistake" thing
    The crime committed was reprehensible,
    Should investigate and act responsible,
As protesters attacked the U. S. Embassy in Beijing

Perlez reported that China, rather than veto, might delay a UN Security Council solution for Kosovo in retaliation for bombing its embassy in Belgrade. Chines Ambassador, Qin Huasun, said that a halt to air strikes was a precondition for discussion.

The bombing endangered congressional approval of China's entry into the WTO. Congress was still miffed over allegations of Chinese espionage of U. S. "missile and nuclear technology."

Milosevic announced a partial removal of troops from Kosovo, but bombing escalated anyway. Albright shrugged off Milosevic's announcement as a "half measure." Clinton was somewhat encouraged, however, but stuck to his original demands.

Eckholm penned the Chinese government said most anti-American protests were elaborately staged but controlled in a national display of unity. Government offices and organizations throughout China were ordered to participate in meetings and issue denunciations over the bombing of its embassy in Belgrade. University students and faculty and private and state companies were allowed to send volunteer delegations. Even Buddhist monks, Tibetan monks, Taoist, Catholic, Protestant and Muslim leaders marched in obedience.

NATO's bombing of China's Embassy in Belgrade angered protesters that forced Kentucky Fried Chicken outlets to close, called off an investment conference and vacated an office building for "security reasons." The anti-American protests worried American foreign investors.

Foreign-backed companies produced nearly half of China's exports, created many jobs and invested $46 million in 1998. China needed a constant flow of foreign investments to keep its economy growing.

NATO rebuffed plans from Russia and China to halt missile air attacks on Yugoslavia wrote Myers and Gordon. It would continue air bombardment until Milosevic removed all troops from Kosovo, allowed Albanian Muslims to return and permitted an international security force to "peacefully invade" its sovereign borders.

Defense Secretary Cohen rejected any partial withdrawal of Serbian forces from Kosovo as unacceptable. He said, "It would be a total victory for Milosevic." NATO and Pentagon officials both agreed that partial withdrawal of forces was a sham, since nearly 30,000 Serbian troops would remain.

After four days of protests in Beijing, U. S. Ambassador Sasser left the American Embassy reported the Associated Press. He walked to a guarded apartment complex that housed diplomats and foreign journalists.

On the same day, the remains of the three Chinese journalists killed in the bombing of its embassy in Belgrade were returned to China. More than 20 diplomats and staff members returned to communist China as well.

As a byproduct of the Chinese Embassy bombing, the meeting between China Construction Bank and Goldman Sachs and Company was canceled. Five Kentucky Fried Chicken and three McDonalds' restaurants were also shut down.

Three citizens reacted adversely to "awarding purple hearts" to three POWs who were in the wrong place at the wrong time, but not wounded in combat. Military W. W. II purple heart veteran Ross called contemplated awards an "insult to those wounded in combat with the enemy," but didn't blame the POWs.

Citizen Doyle noted that many POWs returned home quietly without media fanfare. He felt "insulted" because he earned his medals "the hard way" as a Vietnam veteran. The POWs were not heroes in his eyes.

Citizen Jansen thought that Clinton was incompetent to lead
Lacked the skill and used his favorite "cover-up"—media feed
    After China's Embassy was bombed in error,
    His minions blamed Milosevic on the air,
When "intelligence" used "out-dated" maps in the dastardly deed

Gordon's column conveyed that Lieutenant General Short, NATO's top air commander, pressed for increased air attacks on Kosovo. He also echoed statements by General Clark who said, "Serbian troops must be killed and Milosevic must accept NATO's terms of capitulation." He took pains not to criticize NATO diplomats and their notions of "constrained bombing limits." General Short preferred "bombing the heart of Milosevic's operation."

Apparently, General Short was "obeying orders like a good soldier" and trying to accomplish what had never been accomplished, i. e., "and win a war by air bombardment alone."

Citizen Wasserman called Clinton's War a consequence of following Albright's advice, since her fingerprints were all over the disaster. He believed that regardless of the "kingdom come bombing" of the Serbs, they would continue to fight for Kosovo. Wasserman accused Clinton of "not having a foreign policy brain."

Pearson, another citizen, observed that large minorities dwelling in Serbia don't work out well. The minorities "want autonomy or even demand independence on the grounds of discrimination and repression— real or imagined."

(The author reasoned years ago in his 1997 book, "The Clintons' Agenda for Change: Assault on Traditional America" and in his 1999 book, "Clinton's Planned Betrayal of America "UNAmericanization" that Clinton's plan to multiculturize the U. S. through an "open borders and lax immigration control" policies were congruent with ultimate "desovernization and denationalization everywhere" directly in concert with his primary global government objective.)

NATO bombed a village near Prizren that resulted in more than 79 deaths and 58 injuries according to Urosevic, a Prizren police office scribed Erlanger. Markings of various bomb stabilizer fins showed NATO markings.

NATO was still investigating to determine if their "misdirected bombs" caused the killing of refugees, many of them children. "Estimates of the exact number of deaths and injured were difficult because Albanians took the dead away," said Dr. Softic of Prizren hospital.

Hobler echoed NATO's claim that about 87 Albanians had been killed in Kosovo because they were used as shields around military targets near Korisa. Pentagon's Bacon called the use of Albanian shields a means of turning world opinion against NATO. The Serbs denied the allegation and retorted that NATO was using "collateral deaths" to prove that only it could return the refugees to Kosovo. Bacon added that the "collateral deaths and injuries" would not shake NATO's resolve and air strikes would continue with increasing force.

Reverend Jesse Jackson criticized the "conduct of the war" and warned that it may soon develop into a "special moral challenge for this generation" akin to what occurred curing the Vietnam debacle.

Lind's article stressed NATO's defense of legitimate rights as an invasion of a sovereign nation. The article weighed the pros and cons of meddling in the domestic affairs of sovereign nations.

NATO's meddling in the internal affairs of the Serbian nation
Was a struggle between sovereignty and vast ethnic "inundation"
> A massive ethnic presence was used
> To make claims on the country abused
That boldly "demanded its cultural right to self-determination"

NATO's air bombardment was designed as a key "self serving" invasion
Brazenly trampled on the sovereignty of the Serbian nation
> The very idea of a "protectorate"
> A move to "denationalize" inviolate,
That "justified" foreign meddling via "ethnic self-determination"

NATO's "survival and 'legitimate' meddling" in the domestic affairs of nations
Mirrored U. S. policy of "ethnic autonomy within a sovereign nation"
> Western Europe's "mini one-world" rule,
> Was the prize at stake that any fool
Could envision with the problem resolved only by Serbia's complete subjugation

As of May 15, 1999, McManus and Marshall wrote that after seven weeks, over 5,000 air sorties and a bombed Chinese Embassy, the results were as follows:

Ethnic cleansing in Kosovo had continued largely unimpeded
The war's end was nowhere in sight, Serb military has not conceded
    Russia was perplexed and China was furious,
    Diplomatic crises festered most injurious,
Since UN Security Council's approval had not yet proceeded

(In reality, "Slick Willie" Clinton dared not seek UN Security Council approval because of possible vetoes from Russia and China. It was essentially the similar ploy clever, conniving Clinton consistently employed when issuing executive orders and federal rules and regulations to "bypass" possible congressional rejections.)

Clinton, Albright and Talbot were feverishly working diplomatically to maintain amicable relations with Russia and China in order to avoid any "major power" confrontation.

Les Gelb, Council of Foreign Relations, saw a period of great strain
'Cause Russia and China desired a bombing halt with its tragic pain
    If the war terminated badly,
    America would suffer sadly
With a loss of "diplomatic armed might prestige" due to Clinton's War bane

A photo op "staged in the oval office" featured "grief-stricken" Clinton signing a condolence book that expressed "regrets" over NATO's bombing of the Chinese Embassy in Belgrade. The column didn't mention if Clinton bit his lower lip during the signing. China's Ambassador Li Zhaoxing and Minister Counselor Liu Xiaoming witnessed the inking.

National Imagery and Mapping Agency, NIMA, and Inaccurate Civilian-Military Maps

Getter's column revealed that the National Imagery and Mapping Agency, NIMA, was the source of a "bad map" in re mistakenly bombing the Chinese Embassy in Belgrade. NIMA and its predecessor have been involved in at least 12 previous "accidents" that resulted in deaths and loss of military aircraft since 1985.

In the past 15 months, NIMA maps were critical in three tragedies that caused 28 deaths. Included were the 20 deaths caused by a Marine Prowler jet that severed gondola cables in Cavalese, Italy, five deaths when a Navy Huey helicopter hit power lines in California's Sequoia National Forest and three deaths from errant bombing of the Chinese Embassy in Belgrade.

NIMA has had numerous problems in supplying critical maps on time to combat pilots. Many of its senior analysts and cartographers had departed, Congressional funding had been deficient and liaison between the "intelligence and defense" departments had been contentious.

The cited "map blunders" showed the Chinese Embassy on the wrong street, failed to show the gondola wires in Calavese, Italy and didn't display the power lines in California's Sequoia National Forest.

The article also noted that the CIA analysts who picked the embassy target and NATO commanders who approved it were remiss in not detecting the map mistake.

Lieutenant General King defended NIMA's overall proficiency. Senator Bob Kerry supported the agency by saying that NIMA had a "lot of satisfied customers."

According to Erlanger, Milosevic was willing to negotiate but not capitulate on any "peace agreement." Mihajlovic, leader of New Democracy, was frustrated at the plodding mediating efforts of Russia's Chernomyrdin. Serbia's sovereignty over Kosovo was the main negotiating point. Russia, however, had to balance its interests against those of Yugoslavia and maintain "good" relations with the West. Negotiations had to be such that Serbia's adversaries were allowed to save face and proclaim victory.

(In the author's view, any international force placed on Serbian soil along with a token Serbian military presence, is a defeat for Milosevic and a victory for imperialistic Clinton, NATO and the United Nations. The admission of foreign troops onto Serbian soil is the "gateway precedence" to gobbling up remaining countries like Romania, Albania, Montenegro and other Western European nations not yet in the fold or under the hegemony of the UN and its murderous, military mechanic, NATO.)

Jesse Jackson's Release of the POWs and White House Consternation

Dowd's column described a frustrated Jesse Jackson because of the shabby treatment accorded him on returning the three POWs to Ramstein AFB and his belated, low key reception at the White House. White House hawks and State Department officials were rather incensed and visibly miffed that he violated protocol, usurped their domain and stole their thunder by getting the POWs released. Jesse had purloined a most coveted, choice White House public relations opportunity.

Jackson's Chicago office was deluged with e-mail and phone calls that implored "Run, Jesse Run." His poll ratings had risen, but at the time, Jesse has not yielded to those calls. Gore, perhaps, was relieved and had for the moment stopped his presidential nominee "one-world" quaking.

Maureen Dowd wrote how Clinton's hawks planned to keep Jesse Jackson in place

> He'd prayed with the Clintons after Bill's adulterous Lewinsky disgrace
> Mad bomber Albright, too, must have been really hot,
> Since Berger sits "de facto" in her Sec-State spot,
> Though Jesse's poll numbers climbed, he wasn't "ready" for the White House race
> Clinton hawks were livid at Jesse for getting the POWs "out"

So they arranged "low grade" receptions that made Reverend Jackson "pout"

    Served him "cold cuts," not dinner, at Ramstein Air Force Base,
    Kept him waiting for an hour to "keep him in his place,"
And didn't meet "Slick" in the Oval Office, a fete he couldn't "tout"

Reverend Jesse Jackson was understandably "miffed"
The "cold cuts" served at Ramstein created the needless "rift"
    A "TV-less" White House reception,
    Caused pause for serious reflection,
Though he got the POWs freed, jealous Clinton felt "stiffed"

Ongoing Peace Negotiations—Beginning of the Thaw

Although peace negotiations were in process, Britain's Foreign Minister Cook proposed NATO sends ground troops into Kosovo without a peace agreement in hopes the refugees could return home by winter. That operation would commence after several more weeks of air bombardment had "softened" Serbian resistance. France, too, supported the use of ground troops.

The White House, however, wary of casualties and domestic dissent, planned to continue air strikes. Italy and Greece were not keen on using ground troops in Kosovo either.

Foreign Minister spokesman, Vujovic, said that Yugoslavia was open to peace initiatives proposed by Russia and seven Western Democracies wrote Donnelly. As a sign of good will, two Serbian POWs held by the U. S. were released to Yugoslavian authorities.

Strains in NATO's 19-member alliance were evident. Germany called the option of using ground troops in Kosovo "unthinkable." Germany should know; they suffered a W. W. II nightmare when they invaded Yugoslavia with numerous German troop divisions locked in a frustrating, stifling stalemate.

Clinton's echo, Britain's Blair, and Italy favored a ground troop invasion of Kosovo. Duplicitous Clinton kept Serbia swinging in the wind by saying, "We have not and will not take any option off the table."

Chernomyrdin, Talbot and Finland's Aktissari had secret peace talks to stop the bombing, if Milosevic capitulated to NATO's demands. Those demands were to withdraw forces from Kosovo, allow international forces in Kosovo and permit the Albanian Muslims to return to Kosovo.

Madigan's column highlighted the main negotiating points in bringing peace to Kosovo. The key elements were that NATO must cease bombing, no international peace force in Kosovo without Milosevic's consent, return of refugees to Kosovo, withdrawal of substantial Serb forces from Kosovo and involvement of Milosevic in negotiating its details.

One possible explanation for the shift in Serbian policy may possibly be attributed to reports of hundreds of Serbian Army reservists deserting from Kosovo.

Meanwhile, strains in NATO were evident. Germany opposed ground troops in Kosovo, Italy demanded an end to the air strike strategy and Greece urged increased efforts for peace negotiated by NATO.

A blurb in the New York Times penned that on a recent visit to Washington, D. C., General Clark told Pentagon officials that 45,000 to 50,000 NATO ground troops needed to be assembled in Macedonia. In a psychological warfare sense, their presence would serve to convince Milosevic to accept NATO's imposed political objectives of capitulation coupled with the use of Apache helicopter gun ships and tougher moves to cut off Yugoslavia's oil. Clark felt that the three-pronged strategy would do the trick.

Meanwhile, Russia's Chernomyrdin, America's Talbot and Finland's Ahtisaari met in an attempt to negotiate a political settlement.

NATO bombed the Dragisa Misovic hospital in Belgrade killing four patients and wounding dozens reported Erlanger. Dr. Sumrad called it an "utterly cynical act by NATO." Dr. Branislava asked, "Why are these patients guilty of anything?" And, "We thought we were safer here than at home."

NATO's Shea remarked that one laser-guided missile "failed to guide correctly." He added that "military targets will continue to be struck and every conceivable measure will be taken to avoid damage to civilian property and harm to civilians."

Sumrak responded tartly to Shea's remarks that "bombing targets 500 yards from a hospital was not taking every conceivable measure to avoid damage; at least not in my opinion."

Serb Health Minister Leposova Milicevic opined that NATO's decision to target the hospital in the wake of dropping a cluster bomb on the grounds of another hospital in Nix two weeks ago was unconscionable. "No medical facility is used by the army or the police," said Milicevic; "I checked it out myself."

The nearby residences of the ambassadors from Spain, Norway and Sweden were also damaged in this "errant" missile attack.

NATO's plan to assign troops for peacekeeping in Kosovo was urged by the White House scribed Perlez. Up to 50,000 troops stationed along Yugoslavia's borders to help refugees return to Kosovo was recommended by NATO. The U. S. would furnish 7,000 troops. The entry of NATO's invasion into Yugoslavia was also possible. Clinton, however, said the build up was intended for peacekeeping and not invasion.

(If the reader recalls, build up of ground forces in Macedonia was voiced previously by Britain, France, Senator McCain, General Clark and others. Perhaps the stage was being set for Clinton to "justify" use of ground troops if the need arose or simply for psychological warfare purposes. No one really knew for sure what Clinton had in mind at the time.)

Diplomats were busy negotiating a deal that would allow a small force of Serbs in Kosovo to protect religious sites, act as tax collectors and as newly formed police. Milosevic would control the small force.

A column by Dahlburg and Drogin detailed another "misdirected" missile attack blunder against KLA Albanian guerrillas housed in their military barracks. Seven rebel fighters were killed and 25 injured according to Milosevic. Ironically, the guerrillas had been placing satellite phone calls reporting Yugoslav Army movements to NATO.

NATO blamed another instance of "bad intelligence" for the mistake. NATO's Shea said, "NATO didn't know it had changed hands." The barracks had recently been in control of the Yugoslavian Army.

Pentagon's Bacon insisted that 50,000 ground troops were necessary as "peace keepers' if the war ended soon. NATO's North Atlantic Council would decide on the matter within a week.

NATO also mistakenly bombed a prison where KLA commanders and other prisoners were jailed. Nineteen prisoners and guards plus a deputy warden were killed. The prison was part of a Serbian military complex—the reason for its targeting.

The British reported that 25,000 sorties were flown; 7,000 were attack missions. NATO planned to continue air bombardment with greater intensity.

Kranish and Cullen also reported their version of the attack on the KLA barracks where seven soldiers were killed and perhaps 15 wounded. Pentagon's Shea told reporters that the mistake occurred because of the belief that it was still occupied by Serbs. Reporters were in "total disbelief" since they had been visiting the barracks for two weeks and their presence was shown regularly on television. KLA's Thaci called the bombing a "tragic mistake" but that NATO attacks must continue.

Meanwhile, NATO was busy bombing in a devastating attack on Serbis's electric power system. Sixteen cities lost power when graphite bombs short-circuited some electric transformers and "soft or ordinary" bombs destroyed others. The purpose of eliminating electric power was to impose hardship on both civilians and the military and to encourage capitulation.

Yugoslavian forces also released 2,000 Albanians from prison originally considered as terrorists.

Serbia was forcing more Albanian Muslims living in Pristina and Urosevac to leave reported Rhode. Food supplies were then sparse in

Kosovo. UN's Redmond said the Serbs were "getting more serious about expelling people."

Trains in Pristina and Urosevac were loaded with refugees bound for Macedonia. In order to make room, 2,000 refugees per day were flown out to western European countries and the United States.

Citizen Goldstein, W. W. II veteran did not perceive the three POWs as heroes. They never served in combat and in no way distinguished them. He did respect the fact the trio of POWs "admitted they were not heroes."

Los Angeles Fetes the POWs as Heroes

Regardless of misperceiving the POWs as "heroes" and because two of them were Hispanic, local politicians played on the public's emotions and seized a "favorable" political opportunity to make themselves look good. Los Angeles Mayor Riordan, civic organizations, council members and even the clergy spent countless hours, energy and money mistakenly proclaiming them as "heroes" and not victims and even gave them a parade.

Goldstein decried the fact that millions of service personnel who were killed, cruelly treated and maimed as POWs, some still patients in veterans' hospitals, never received civic adulation, acclaim, public or media attention as these POWs. He opined that local politicians and civic organizations had to be desperate searching for heroes!

Citizen Horvitz recalled more injuries he'd seen in navy boot camp during W. W. II than these three POWs received during containment. He said, "To give them Purple Hearts was as 'insult' to those veterans who 'earned' them."

Horvitz said each POW deserved the country's gratitude for conducting themselves like any good soldier was expected to behave as a captive. He thought they were probably awed at being called "heroes."

Bombing Beat Goes On—Air Strikes Continue Relentlessly

NATO continued to bomb relentlessly Serbia's electric and water supply that was seriously affecting the daily life of ordinary citizens reported Erlanger. Food could not be refrigerated or cooked before eating, milk not warmed for babies and pure water drank with safety. Batteries and bottled water were rapidly selling out in the stores.

City officials in Belgrade said that homes lacked running water or the power to run electric motors to pump water. Most homes in Belgrade have electric water heaters. New water cannot be filtered and only 30 percent of residents had running water.

A UN report claimed that as many as 150,000 refugees were headed for Macedonia wrote Kratovac. The numbers of sexual violence committed against Albanian women was perhaps insensitively described so the UN's immediate remedy was to send "morning after" pills. The assertions were based on interviews of 35 female refugees.

At the same time, NATO bombarded Milosevic's villa, military barracks and other targets. It also repeated its intent to amass 50,000 "peace keepers," perhaps for eventual duty in Kosovo.

Due to Clinton's inept, myopic planning and constant reduction of the U. S. military during his presidential tenure, reliance on military reservists was already straining demands in Kosovo. The Pentagon ordered a halt on "retirements" for Air Force personnel until Clinton's War ended. The directive was effective June 15, 1999 and could affect 120,000 personnel. As per the directive, at least 600 pilots would be prevented from "leaving the service or retiring." On the other hand, personnel serving in the Army, Navy and Marine Corps were unaffected by the directive.

Dorning's column described growing congressional dissatisfaction with Clinton's air war. House Democrats called for a three-day pause in the bombing to open the door to a peace settlement. The group planned to send a letter to Clinton requesting the pause. Congressmen Clement and

Blagojevich said the epistle would bear the signatures of 21House members. "To escalate or negotiate is the decision," said Blagojevich, "Give them a chance."

Milosevic and Four Aides Indicted as War Criminals and Peace Feelers

A duly appointed International Criminal Tribunal would formally indict Milosevic as a war criminal wrote Cohen. The only remaining task was to arrest and bring him to trial. Louise Armour, chief prosecutor for the International Criminal Tribunal revealed that the "inquiry against Milosevic began in 1993."

Milosevic countered the charge with his own. He asserted that NATO's bombings was an act of genocide itself, which caused thousands of Albanian Muslims to flee Kosovo,

Chernomyrdin commented that this decision to indict Milosevic would undermine the negotiating process. Germany's Steiner said, "There is no point complaining or applauding."

Milosevic and four aides (Mulitonovic, Sainovic, Ojdanic and Strojilkovic) were indicted by the International Criminal Tribunal of personal responsibility for the persecution, deportation and murders of hundreds of thousands of Albanian Muslims forcefully ejected from Kosovo wrote Vrazo. Chief Prosecutor, French-Canadian Louise Armour, charged them with 248 named deaths and 740,000 ejected refugees.

Clinton praised the timely diversionary action of the tribunal. It meant that Milosevic couldn't travel outside of Yugoslavia to any UN nation for fear of arrest. Only a special UN Security Council Order could grant him immunity to attend a peace conference outside of Yugoslavia.

Milosevic's arrest in Yugoslavia was considered unlikely since the tribunal failed to arrest any war criminals indicted in the Bosnian War.

Yugoslavian officials dismissed the indictment as a ploy to justify continued air bombardment for over two months. The Serbs said they attacked the KLA to end guerrilla attacks on Serbian forces.

Meanwhile, the bombing raged on and Serbian forces continued their "ethnic cleansing" campaign.

Clinton's War in Kosovo caused his poll ratings to drop to 53 percent noted an anonymously written Associated Press item. People were concerned about peace after nine weeks of air strikes and talk of a ground invasion. The public was less supportive of Clinton's War and Clinton himself.

The response from U. S. National Security Council's Hammer was immediate. He insisted that NATO's provisions for peace were not negotiable.

Chernomyrdin believed the sticking points in the NATO-Serbian peace negotiations were that the same nations made up the international peace keepers and commanded the force and the size of Yugoslavian Army and police units allowed to stay in Serbia's province, Kosovo. He expected to have further discussions with Finland's Ahtisaari and one-worlder, Strobe Talbot. Talbot made it plain that Russia's envoy wouldn't represent NATO or the U. S.

Myers described how Defense Secretary Cohen and counterparts in Britain, France, Germany and Italy met in Germany to discuss how large a force would be needed to invade Serbia. General Clark thought 150,000 troops would suffice. Britain would contribute 50,000 troops, but other details were kept secret.

The five defense secretaries agreed to NATO Secretary General Solana's request to enlarge and intensify the air bombardment because "it was working" and moved immediately to place 50,000 peacekeepers on Kosovo's borders.

Milosevic offered NATO a limited peacekeeping role in Kosovo via talks with Chernomyrdin scribed Boudreaux and Dahlburg. Details of the plan were:

(a)   Reduce Serbian forces in Kosovo, permit over-flights and Russian reconnaissance planes to validate the withdrawal,

(b)   Have a military officer from a neutral nation command the force with the force reporting to the UN Security Council. NATO staff from non-bombing countries would assist,

(c) Have troops from Russia and its confederation of states escort refugees and maintain peace in Kosovo. Troops from NATO bombing nations could patrol Kosovo's border areas,

(d) Deploy troops from 10 NATO bombing nations in Macedonia and Albania to assist the refugees' return,

(e) Withdraw NATO forces from neighboring countries before Serbian troops leave Kosovo

France's Chirac and Germany's Schroeder asked for a G-8 meeting to assess the plan. Supreme NATO commander, General Clark, called the plan "a thrust for a bombing pause." Britain's Foreign Secretary Cook thought the bombing pressure was getting to Milosevic.

Meanwhile, the Pentagon ordered 68 more aircraft into Clinton's War. When stationed, NATO would have 1,000 warplanes, mostly from the U. S. (Surprise, surprise, "nine" NATO nations had "not" contributed any military aircraft to fight Clinton's War.)

Yugoslavia claimed nine civilians were killed and 28 wounded in an air attack on a bridge in Yarvarin wrote Schmitt. NATO promptly and sheepishly claimed no civilians were visible on the bridge at the time of the attack.

"Collateral attacks" on civilian infrastructure like electric power plants that furnish electricity to hospitals and water-pumping stations had impelled Italy and Greece to call for a halt in bombing as an inducement for Milosevic to capitulate.

General Clark rejected that suggestion and said that bombings, not a moratorium, would urge Milosevic to submit to NATO's demands. At the time, no Serbian signs of surrender existed.

During a Memorial Day address delivered at Arlington National Cemetery, Vietnam draft dodger Clinton said, "The motive for bombing Kosovo was to save lives—including American lives" related Broder. He expected the U. S. to contribute 7,000 troops as part of 50,000 peace-keepers in Macedonia, available for duty in Kosovo. Clinton declared that

Europeans would furnish most troops. Clinton was cognizant of the fact that "most Americans believed that Kosovo was not our fight."

"Slick" Clinton knew that Kosovo "wasn't ever" America's fight
National security was never at risk in this bombing plight
    Tried to make the case for intervention,
    "If we'd acted with the same intention
In W. W. II, "rows of white crosses wouldn't be present or in sight"

(Of course, the master of spin doctoring, revisionist Clinton, among other omissions, failed to mention that Japan sneakily attacked Pearl Harbor amid ongoing "peace" negotiations and President Roosevelt immediately declared war on Japan on that "day of infamy." In Clinton's War, Serbia never attacked the U. S. or had a one world objective as did Japan, the then soon-to-be willing accomplice of the "Axis.")

Clinton repeated the five demands for ending the aerial destruction of military and civilian facilities in Serbia. He emphasized the presence of peacekeepers in Kosovo "with NATO at its core."

"Left and right" domestic critics of Clinton charged that vital security or economic risks to the U. S. from Yugoslavia never existed. Clinton retorted lamely to the criticism with a fatuous generalization, "We have a greater capacity to bear a large share of the burden!" "This is something we, the U. S. and European military, have done together."

Eranger scribed that 16 civilian and 43 civilians were wounded in missile attacks on a hospital in Surdulica. Ten more were killed and 20 wounded in air attacks on a TV station and apartment building in Pazar. Two people died and eight were wounded on a bridge between Leskovac and Lebane by air bombardment.

More daylight and intensified air attacks were continuing mercilessly to bring Milosevic to his knees. Meanwhile, Yugoslavia had accepted the G-8's principles of peace. It had accepted the idea of NATO troops in the force, but preferred to have troops participate from non-bombing countries in Kosovo, U. S. troops excluded.

Chapter 6

Peace Proposal Acceptance and Aftermath

Details of Clinton's War discussed chronologically include Milosevic's Acceptance of the Peace Proposal, The Pull Out Plan, Provisions of the Peace Plan, Serbia Signs the Peace Pact as Clinton Crows, Confirmation of Serbian Troop Withdrawal from Kosovo, Russia and the Pristina Airport Affair, KLA Reactions, Reluctance and Dominance after Serbian Troop Withdrawal and Criticisms and Costs of Clinton's War. As usual, other pertinent events are interspersed chronologically among the major headings.

Milosevic's Acceptance of the Peace Proposal

Cohen reported that Milosevic was ready to withdraw forces from Kosovo and accept a UN presence there. He wanted an immediate end to air strikes as a condition for peace.

Finnish president, Ahtisaari, carried a detailed peace settlement plan and would meet with Milosevic. The move was viewed as a prelude to the Serbian leader buckling under tremendous air strike pressures and perhaps fearing the possibility of a ground war with NATO forces.

Meanwhile, Clinton and his Joint Chiefs of Staff, "without apparently in disfavor" General Clark, would meet to discuss options for using troops in a possible invasion.

Secretary of State Albright said, "We will not settle for less," that is, "withdrawal of all Serb forces from Kosovo, an international force with NATO at its core in Kosovo and the return of nearly one million Albanian Muslim refugees."

Italy's foreign minister Dini agreed that acceptance of NATO-imposed conditions must precede cessation of air strikes—a reversal of Italy's previous position to halt bombings first.

Clinton delivered the commencement address to the 1999 graduating class of the USAF Academy and urged Milosevic to "accept the peace deal and cut his losses." He told the cadets the air campaign was succeeding and would prevail; otherwise, Serbia would become economically and militarily ruined.

The U. S. would contribute 7,000 troops that would serve as peace-keepers, mine cleaners, road builders and provide shelter for refugees.

Clinton responded to critics that suggested removal of human rights observers and the start of air strikes caused thousands of Albanian Muslims to flee Kosovo. He evaded a direct answer to the question and said that the air bombardment "was planned for months" because the Serbs had massacred civilian Albanian Muslims in Rajac in January 1999. In effect "for the world's ears only," Clinton said, "The tragedy would have continued and been condoned by the world had we done nothing."

A "softened" peace deal was offered to Milosevic in order to bring peace wrote Donnelly. The "softeners" included allowing nominal numbers of Serbian police along Kosovo's borders and at Customs, labeling the peace-keepers as a UN force even if NATO controlled them and halting the air strikes after withdrawal of forces from Kosovo became clearly evident.

Previous demands dropped from the peace pact were creation of only one police force, the Organization of Security and Cooperation in Europe (OSCE) and only OSEC police in towns and at Customs offices.

Serbian police would participate in all activities and have the right to search OSCE vehicles.

Milosevic accepted the peace plan to end Clinton's War on June 3, 1999, 72 days after air strikes began on March 24, 1999 reported Erlanger. He agreed to withdraw all military and police forces within seven days and allow 50,000 thousand international troops under UN aegis to police Kosovo. Details would be worked out among military leaders from both sides.

One of Yugoslavia's ministers, Matic, said that NATO must honor its commitment to "demilitarize the KLA." NATO's indirect response was that "a credible and verifiable withdrawal of Serb forces must occur first, however, before air attacks cease."

Chernomyrdin and NATO succeeded in negotiating the peace proposal. Only 1,000 Serb "police" would be allowed to enter Kosovo to guard key border posts and holy religious sites. "Kosovo would become autonomous with substantial loss of Serbian sovereignty over it."

Clinton warned Milosevic to accept the recent peace deal
"Cut your losses now" or we'll force you to reel
　　Serbia will become more devastated,
　　Its firm economic structure "wasted,"
With military destruction—no matter how you feel

Erlangers's column described Clinton's War as a "war of miscalculation from the start."

Clinton assumed that after a short period of missile-bombing strikes
The Serb nation would capitulate like a bunch of frightened little "tikes"
　　Erred on Kosovo's geopolitical meaning
　　And Serbia's true religious-cultural leaning,
To "save face and NATO," pulverized Serbia, disdained critics' dislikes

Milosevic, too, made several unfortunate miscalculations
Thought huge civilian casualties would "incite" other nations
    Assumed NATO might go asunder,
    Turned out to be another blunder,
As did the flood of refugees into poor Border States' dislocations

Politically astute Milosevic finally capitulated when 1200 civilian deaths occurred from "misguided missile accidents" and the "votes for peace" rendered by his legislative body. He felt that remaining in power and knowing that he survived NATO's 19-nation "hi-tech" forces without demoralization, no panic and no mass desertions was a victory in itself. He also surmised that loss of electric power and heating plants, along with the coming cold winter, would cause unrest. Many factories had been destroyed. Jobs were lost and most highways, bridges and Serbia's only two refineries damaged or destroyed. It was feared that a civilian rebellion against his government might occur. Historian Djilas opined that "Western public opinion had proved less humane and will tolerate 'high civilian casualties—on the enemy's side' and 'few on its own.'"

An interim international authority would govern Kosovo, establish "democratic institutions and elections" and rebuild the infrastructure. Albanian Muslims and Serb Christians were expected to work out a long-term political solution with sovereignty for Kosovo as proposed at Rambouillet.

Yugoslavia's Radical Party, led by Sesely, swore to quit the government the day NATO troops entered Kosovo. Historian Cosic called the peace deal "an extorted decision, a matter of survival and not a matter of freedom and rights."

A cautious Clinton was relieved that Milosevic had agreed to the peace proposal wrote Broder and Perlez. Clinton and some of his staff were still skeptical, however. Air bombardment would continue until Serbian forces actually withdrew from Kosovo. NATO troops would move immediately into Kosovo after Serbian forces departed.

Critics in and out of Congress charged Clinton with starting a war on a foreign nation that "did not threaten U. S. interests." Nevertheless, victory or more accurately "cessation of hostilities" by air strikes seemed on the edge of success.

Clinton made an offer to Milosevic that he "couldn't refuse"
Accept "our peace proposal or Serbia becomes "total refuse"
> Allow international forces in,
> Let refugees return to where they'd been,
As another blow was struck against "nationalism to defuse"

"Veep" Albert Gore was pleased Clinton's War wouldn't affect his presidential campaign
> "No U. S. troops fighting in a European War" was a benefit he would gain
>> State's Rubin wasn't ready to pop champagne corks,
>> He preferred to wait until the "forced peace plan" works,
> Secretary of State Albright was guardedly satisfied; "it prolonged her reign"

According to Mitchell, Clinton was "anxious to end the bombing" in Yugoslavia, and the Pentagon anticipated the end of the war—if Serb troops left Kosovo. Clinton sought to convince Americans that the war was worth it, i. e., stabilizing Europe, returning 800,000 Albanian Muslims to their mainly non-existent homes and constructing a prosperous "democratic" Balkan region.

As the bombing continued to strike military targets but not Belgrade, NATO and Serbian commanders were discussing a timetable for withdrawal of forces as Serbs and the KLA continued to fight sporadically.

NATO prepared to send in international forces into Kosovo, but suspended deployment of 36 F-15 fighters to Turkey.

Thus far, NATO's casualties had been astoundingly "zero" and Clinton's prolonged air war had been successful, notwithstanding the fact that Milosevic still remained in power.

Senator McCain contended that Clinton's War guaranteed that Milosevic would remain in power. Jesse Helms wanted the president to seek congressional approval before sending troops into Kosovo, else he would hold up Holbrooke's nomination as chief diplomat to the United Nations.

Schmitt and Gordon wrote that NATO commanders believed air power alone had bent Milosevic's will by bombing mercilessly military and civilian structures. General Clark said it was due to precise bombing weaponry, avoidance of losses, increased destruction of Serb forces and generously added "luck."

Perhaps even the threat of a standby army of nearly 50,000 NATO sited in Macedonia played a significant role, too.

NATO's bombing callously spurned criticism of "collateral damage" (civilian deaths and injuries and destruction of Serbia's infrastructure). At the beginning of Clinton's War, General Clark was uncertain that air power alone could succeed. Just two days ago, many American and NATO generals still thought similarly.

Two mistakes due to "political considerations" that should have been avoided were "not to bomb Belgrade aimed at shocking the Serbian people and Clinton promising never to use ground forces." Without doubt, the two errors prolonged capitulation. Later, Clinton praised talk of using ground troops, perhaps spurring Milosevic to bend. Originally, NATO diplomats, Albright, Berger and Cohen "erroneously" concurred with Clinton on the strategy that a few days of intense bombing would force Milosevic's immediate capitulation.

The "Pull Out" Plan

British Lieutenant General Jackson met with the Serbs at Blace, a border checkpoint, and delivered the terms for a verifiable withdrawal of 40,000 Serbian troops from Kosovo to his Serb counterparts wrote Cullen and Leonard. The plan would "begin the pull out within 24 hours and finish in seven days, then air strikes would cease."

Some of the terms of peace included withdrawal of the Serbian regular army, armed civilian groups, national border guards, military, anti-terrorist police and intelligence services. Additionally, the Serbian Air Force, air defense, aircraft radar, surface-to-air missiles and anti-aircraft artillery had to be removed swiftly. Lastly, information on location and type of land mines was required to be disclosed.

The standby international force of peacekeepers stationed in Macedonia consisted of 12,000 British, 7,000 Americans, 5,000 French and other troops from Germany, Italy and other "non NATO" countries. The KFOR was ready to invade Serbia's province, Kosovo, although Russian troops would not be under NATO" command according to Chernomyrdin.

Two days of "negotiable peace plans" failed to finalize details for a withdrawal of Serbian forces from Kosovo scribed Becker. NATO's merciless air strikes would continue until Serbia capitulated.

Stumbling blocks that persisted in arriving at agreement were "no guarantee for the safe return of refugees and full withdrawal of all Serbian forces from Kosovo" according to Lieutenant General Jackson. Another impediment was "the full respect of sovereignty and territorial integrity of Yugoslavia" as per Bujovic, Yugoslavia's deputy foreign minister.

Yugoslavian representatives said they needed 48 hours to remove anti aircraft defense and have NATO clear out land mines. The buffer zone between the borders of Kosovo with Macedonia and with Serbian and Russian troops stationed at the northern border of Kosovo remained sticking points.

Peace talks stalled after Russia objected to any of its troops serving under NATO control scribed Perlez. They insisted to the UN that they have a role in peacekeeping. A request by Yugoslavia to keep 15, 000 troops in Kosovo was rejected as unacceptable by the State Department.

Meanwhile, military talks in Macedonia were delayed, and NATO promised to intensify air bombardment.

Provisions of the Peace Plan

At present, Britain, Canada, France, Germany, Italy, Japan and the U. S. plus Russia signed the Cologne plan to "invade" Serbia with ground troops wrote Apple, Jr. Russia was less objectionable to certain provisions of the peace pact and preferred its troops serve along Kosovo's northern border under UN not NATO command. A footnote in the plan did not have NATO at the "core of peace keepers" and the chain of command would not be under control of NATO's nation but in "consult" with other non-NATO countries.

Serbia decided that its Customs officials would be positioned on the border crossings to keep non- refugees, "illegal," terrorists and other undesirables out. American officials adamantly opposed a Serbian presence at the border crossings. Eventually, "peace keepers" would control the borders anyway.

At present, 7,000 U. S., perhaps 10,000 Russian and 17,000 troops from Britain, Germany et al were already in Macedonia. In time as many as 53,000 peacekeepers would be stationed in Kosovo. The plan called for "substantial ratio participation" in NATO led forces. Provisions of the peace plan included:

(a) A verifiable, phased pull out of all military police and paramilitary forces from Kosovo,

(b) Full cooperation from all commands including the peace keepers,

(c) Demilitarization of the KLA,

(d) Installation of an international administration and police force to "govern" autonomous Kosovo and

(e) Safe return of 860,000 Albanian Muslims to Kosovo

A well-armed international force of peace keepers was primed to enter Kosovo. British paratroopers and Ghurkas would be in the vanguard of the invasion to halt and/or reverse "ethnic cleansing." Britain had 6,000 troops in Macedonia at the time, destined to grown to 13,000. The U. S.

S. Kearsarge, positioned just off the coast of Macedonia, had 2,200 Marines aboard poised to embark.

The main body of troops would include German, French, Italian, British and U. S. forces from "Big Red One," the lst Infrantry Division. The troops would be heavily armed with Abrams tanks, Bradley Infantry Fighting Vehicles, ground rockets and field artillery.

Serbia Signs the Peace Pact as Clinton Crows

Yugoslavia's military leaders signed a peace pact on June 9, 1999 in which they agreed to leave Kosovo. Colonel Marjanovic said, "It means the war had ended." Serbia had eleven days to withdraw all troops. The UN Security Council was expected to sign a resolution outlining the steps to end the war. NATO Secretary General Solana said, "NATO forces could enter Kosovo once withdrawal of Serbian troops was verified." Lieutenant General Jackson would command IFOR (or KFOR for Kosovo) known as the international force.

Clinton stated that a unified NATO would be in charge. He also warned the KLA not to interfere with the withdrawal of Serbian troops from Kosovo.

The agreement called for all Serbian forces to withdraw from Kosovo within 11 days. All aircraft, radar, surface-to-air and anti-aircraft batteries had to be cleared out within three days. Yugoslavia must supply NATO with maps of land mine placements, booby traps and related. Non-adherence to peace pact provisions would lead immediately to resumption of air bombardment.

Citizen Felburg wondered why "we" just didn't kill Milosevic and let the Serbs work their way out of their Stone Age environment. He wondered if spending billions to destroy Yugoslavia and planning to spend billions more to reconstruct it was just a bribe to oust Milosevic constituted good strategy.

Felburg didn't think the war stopped the killing, raping, looting, burning and ethnic cleansing of Albanian Kosovars.

Clinton declared that NATO had "achieved victory" in his war in Kosovo; however, Yugoslavia would receive no U. S. reconstruction help until Milosevic was removed from power related Schmemann. It was an offer that the Yugoslavian people might find difficult to refuse.

Clinton, "magnanimous" in victory in Kosovo, declared
"Yugoslavia would receive no rebuilding aid to be shared
     Unless Milosevic was removed from power,
     Such assistance United States would not shower,
But use it as blackmail; thus Clinton's arrogance was bared

Clinton's success in Serbia made many military and political experts who never believed that air power alone would win a war appear as incompetent. Fools or not, 50,000 ground troops would still be required to maintain a "78-day air bombardment induced peace." By no politically wishful means, however, would the air war victory resolve centuries of cultural-religious-political hatreds.

It was glaringly obvious that many months of "peaceful" diplomatic negotiations engineered by one-world experts Albright, Holbrooke, Talbot and others had been largely ineffective; else 78 days of air strikes would have been unnecessary.

Clinton crowed about the "solidarity" of NATO's 19 countries. It remained "unified" in conducting the air campaign, even though 10 nations contributed token, nada, zilch, zero or nil to the effort. In hindsight, he tried to justify the air strikes if only Milosevic had capitulated early on to NATO's meddling in Serbia's internal affairs and civil war. Also, Clinton did not mention the series of failed attempts at peaceful negotiations conducted by his expert, diplomatic appointees.

He labeled NATO's efforts as the most difficult challenge in its first "offensive nation meddling" effort. NATO's original "defensive" objective against potential enemy Russia had mysteriously vanished at least temporarily but was scarcely resolved.

Finally, Clinton's statements revealed that the prime motive for meddling in Serbia was to implement a "mini, one world U. S.—Western Europe." He lauded Russia for its help in "resolving" Clinton's War.

Clinton thanked Russia for its "huge help" in Clinton's War resolution
In time, it too would be desired for "mini U. S.—Euro" inclusion
    Formidable challenges still lay ahead,
    Entice other Euro nations to same bed,
Plus "former USSR" nations to complete Western One-World fusion

Clinton, of course, stressed "America's interest in doing our part." He was pleased to announce that the "world did not look away at the misery in Kosovo," which was a bald-faced lie. (In reality, Asia, India, Africa, South America, Central America, the Caribbean, Near East and many other nations contributed absolutely nothing in moral, military or any other assistance toward resolving Clinton's War. Other "uninvolved" nations comprise over an estimated 5.6 billion of the world's population, while the U. S. and European nations "involved" in Clinton's War have a combined estimated population of slightly over 600 million people. Still, the "spin doctoring" goes on.")

Clinton's War in Kosovo had set "precedence and justification"
To "meddle-interfere" in the affairs of any "reluctant" nation
    Sets U. S. policy to "entangle"
    Its might in any "internal wrangle"
And "force" its rule on "nations-in-name-only," one-world capitulation

Confirmation of Serbian Troop Withdrawal from Kosovo

NATO ceased air strikes after confirming Yugoslavia's withdrawal of 40,000 troops from Kosovo had begun 12 hours after the peace agreement was signed wrote Whitney. NATO's Solana stated the cessation of hostilities was the "result of intense diplomacy by many countries including Russia." (What rubbish? Bombing, Serbian legislature's "votes for peace," civilian hardships expected from the ensuing cold winter , Milosevic's political survival and not diplomacy brought Milosevic to his knees.")

Both sides claimed victory. Britain's Blair crowed that "our cause was just and rightly upheld." Chirac said, "A page has been turned in the conflict." The UN passed a resolution by a 14—0 vote to place Kosovo under international civilian control and authorized international peacekeepers known as IFOR.

Russia vehemently opposed the air bombardment and refused to place its troops under NATO's command.

NATO would not tolerate non-compliance to peace terms by either side warned NATO's Solana. He promised the alliance and other international countries would aid in rebuilding a nation freed from repression.

In the parlance of the underworld, NATO had now officially become a "self-appointed mechanic through IFOR," a militant, aggressor institution without reservation. It appeared ready to "impose peace" even if has to "bomb the hell out of any recalcitrant sovereign nation"—that it deemed safe to encounter.

Germany's "Schoeder Plan" intended to re-build Serbia. The six or seven nations plus Russia, agreed to contribute $5 billion to $6 billion annually for many years and raise the Balkans to an economic and social development level equal to the rest of Europe.

NATO troops entered Pristina, capital of Kosovo on June 12, 1999 but Russian troops were already there wrote Kifner and Lee. NATO had planned to make Pristina its headquarters. British troops had already secured the high ground overlooking the highway to Pristina.

Albanian Muslims happily greeted NATO forces comprised of British, Italian, French, and U. S. troops. Cheers went up for the KLA, too. Boos, however, were directed at Macedonian police, which had abused refugees.

Serbian Christians welcomed the Russian troops who had come from Bosnia. They wore the KFOR insignia, the initials of Kosovo involvement.

NATO forces continued to roll into Kosovo. Even Germany's parliament authorized deployment of 8,500 troops.

The formidable problems of what to do about Russian troops, Serbia's rebels, refugees and the role of the KLA still had to be resolved.

Citizen Allred observed that pretentious, hypocrite Clinton implied Hollywood might be responsible for rampant violence—then signed an executive order committing the U. S. to mercilessly bombard Serbia. He thought Slick Willie should "be impeached for committing violence on people in Montenegro, Kosovo and Belgrade, not for lying about sexual peccadilloes."

Citizen Kujawsky opined that justice would not be served until Milosevic, Karodzic, Mladic and other indicted torturers and murderers were brought before the International War Crimes Tribunal.

Another citizen, Mazenko, wondered whether Milosevic or NATO committed the greater war crimes when tens of thousands of Yugoslavians would die due to starvation, cold and disease during winter 1999.

Russian Troops and the Pristina Airport Affair

An anonymous news item described how 300 Russian troops had dug in at the Pristina Airport and commandeered Serbian soldiers and police patrolling the streets. It was evident that "other" NATO forces were clearly not in charge. Serbian forces were expected to withdraw within 11 days, but General Clark said it might take longer. NATO's forces moved cautiously into Kosovo because land mine-clearing teams had to function first.

The Russian decision to seize Pristina's Airport was a military one that Yeltsin himself ordered. The Russians demanded a separate zone and control of their forces within Kosovo. The demand sent Clinton to the "hot phone" and Talbot scurrying to Moscow.

Shenon's column related that phone talks between Bill and Boris failed to resolve the NATO-Russian troop standoff at Pristina Airport. They agreed that military commanders should resolve the matter. General Clark, however, said that negotiations were really "a political problem first and foremost." He added that the problem was "non-military."

The White House tried to "play the matter down." Albright thought, "I think they (Russians) got a little bit ahead of themselves with some political confusion."

Kifner's account of the "impasse at Pristina Airport" blocked entry of British troops and raised some irritation in their commanders. They had previously selected the airport as their headquarters, now were seeking an alternate site.

Meanwhile, long columns of NATO troops continued to invade Kosovo. British paratroopers, German soldiers and unidentified Albanians who fired for unknown reasons killed a number of Serbs.

NATO military officers seethed and left the airport controversy up to the diplomats and politicians. In the meantime, Russian soldiers, aided by Yugoslavian soldiers, blocked the entry road to the airport and many Yugoslavian soldiers were still legally in Kosovo.

Many Serbs were packing up and joining tractor and cart convoys and helped each other with belongings as they prepared to leave the area. On leaving, they burned many buildings.

Eddy's column described NATO's peacekeeper invasion of Kosovo and discovering 81 newly dug graves in Kacanik as KFOR spread out to control more of the province. Refugees continued to stream in, while Serbian troops set homes ablaze as they departed. Centuries old hatreds continued to roil.

Russian control of Pristina's airport was downplayed everywhere. British Lieutenant General Jackson insisted the site was not crucial to

KFOR. Politicians, however, were wary that a Russian zone could lead to partition of Kosovo. For whatever reasons, Russia's role in the peace plan had not been "spelled out."

KLA Reactions, Reluctance and Dominance after Serbian Troop Withdrawal

Invading KFOR numbered up to 15,000 troops and Serbian forces continued to withdraw from Kosovo according to schedule. The KLA offered some resistance to disarming and set up an office in Pristina. KLA leader Thaci said, "It would not guarantee the security of Russians in Kosovo and they were not welcome."

Kifner and Fisher reported NATO forces found many gravesites, toppled mosques, burned homes and ruined shops near DjaKovica, Pec, Bella Crkva and Velika Krusa. Bullet holes were everywhere.

The KLA bases were on the other side of the mountains near Djakovica, the center of Albanian nationalism. Without doubt, the strategic sites probably accounted for the fierce damages and deaths they suffered.

Other cities involved in the devastation were Mala Krusa and Prizren. Many people were massacred and buried in the vicinity and evidence of the atrocities was widespread.

Serbian Orthodox Church officials implored Milosevic to step down for the good of the country along with opposing politicians scribed Gall. The Holy Synod called for new elections and a change in government.

Milosevic ignored the demand and campaigned to remain in office by inspecting bomb damage in Novi Sad and devastation in Mionica. He needed public support to remain in office and complete his tenure that expired in 2000.

Concerned church officials asked KFOR to protect Serbian civilians, orthodox monasteries and churches everywhere. In the meantime, over 3,000 Serbs had fled from Kosovo during the past four days, although their plight was barely shown on television.

U. S. Marines detained six Albanian insurgents and confiscated AK-47s, mines and rocket propelled grenades from 100 members of the KLA. The KLA had become bolder from the moment they assumed power in Kosovo, i. e., after Serbian troops and police left the premises. The weapons were surrendered after Apache and Cobra helicopter gun ships hovered overhead and U. S. Marines surrounded them. Later, the weapons would be destroyed and the six rebels released.

NATO and KLA officials met to arrange the specifics of "demilitarizing" the rebel army and "converting" some of its members into a civilian police force. General Clark required the KLA to abandon its fortifications, surrender its heavy weapons and disband in two phases within 30 days.

To date, the KLA demonstrated reluctance to break up, since it was then the dominating political-military force in Kosovo. The KLA had taken over villages and towns and openly patrolled the streets.

NATO commanders desired to be even-handed by protecting Albanian Muslims and Serbian Christians in like fashion. Nevertheless, Serbians viewed the Albanian rebels as terrorists and had become more anxious since the Serbian Army withdrew.

Six days after 78 days of air bombardment halted on June 17, 1999, officials estimated that at least 10,000 people were murdered in Serbia's "ethnic cleansing" against Albanian Muslims that began on March 24, 1999 wrote King. NATO was concerned Albanian Muslims would seek revenge against Serbian civilians remaining in Kosovo.

Albanian survivors told horror stories of grenades tossed, machine gun fire sprayed wantonly, fires set and threats to kill anyone who might have survived. Some survived by jumping out of windows and running away. A variety of instruments of torture including a pick ax, wooden hats, chains and a black hood were found at the Pristina police station. The Serbian Orthodox Monastery in Decane sheltered Albanian Muslims fleeing from the rampage of withdrawing Serbian soldiers.

Meanwhile, an accord with Russia and their role in Kosovo had not yet been reached. Pentagon's Bacon said that peacekeeping operations would continue—with or without Russian cooperation.

According to Montgomery and Parker, Russia would not be allowed to control its own sector in Kosovo. A tentative agreement was reached where the Russian troops under command of their own officers would report to a Russian officer at NATO Headquarters in Belgium. The officer would then report to Moscow.

Unresolved issues that remained involved daily troop activities and location of Russian troops. In the meantime, the Russians still occupied Pristina's airport.

NATO officials resisted any prominent Russian "packaging role" since it might lead to a portion of Kosovo that favored Serbs!

Clinton, of course, wanted a settlement with Russia for "crowing rights." They had been offered only a small role in peacekeeping. Clinton and two of his one-world policy echoes, Cohen and Albright met with Russia's Sergeyev and Ivanov respectively. Both were confident that the diplomats would resolve the peacekeeping issue.

Sowell worried about Clinton's "quick fix" solution in Kosovo. He raised the issue of possible confrontation with Russian troops, voluntary return of the Kosovar refugees and indefinite presence of U. S. troops in the Balkan tinderbox. The enormous expense of sustaining the U. S. military in the Balkans, high cost of rebuilding Kosovo, Serbian effect on retaining a "voluntary" military and maintaining morale and recruitment were cited as "long range" problems that had been ill-considered by "quick fix" Clinton and like-minded cohorts.

The KLA was installing self-appointed "interim governments" in some cities of Kosovo. Their black uniformed police had taken over municipal buildings and works to provide basic services. Food was considered a major problem.

NATO allowed the KLA the freedom to "deal with local matters" in some areas. In the same vein, its policy to "demilitarize" the KLA was obviously applied haphazardly.

German troops overwhelmed the KLA at a police station where 15 persons (Serbs, Albanians and Gypsies) were held. A badly beaten dead man was found handcuffed to a chair. German troops briefly detained 25 Albanian rebels and confiscated many weapons.

A NATO-Russian deal, subject to NATO's approval, was designed to integrate Russian troops under a unified Western Command. It would incorporate Russian officers into all levels of its command structure. Russia's 3,600 troops would be deployed in three of the five sectors in Kosovo. A separate sector for Russia was denied.

NATO retained overall command, but Russia could decline an order judged unacceptable to Moscow. The solution was similar to the one operating in Bosnia. At the same time, Russia would also have to relinquish control of Pristina's airport.

KLA and NATO commanders reached a tentative agreement to disband all organized military operations scribed Myers. The pact called for the KLA to withdraw from fortified positions, relinquish heavy armament, remove their uniforms and halt organized military operations within a month. NATO's Lieutenant General Jackson and officials at NATO Headquarters would sign the agreement.

After the Serbs removed their military from Kosovo, they would effectively lose control of their sovereignty in the province. Russian troops would control Pristina's airport grounds, not its air traffic, and could deploy troops in the American, German and French sectors of Kosovo.

Costs and Criticisms of the Clinton's War

Several Los Angeles area citizens expressed individual views regarding the effects of Clinton's War.

Marlanadin looked closely at the many things Clinton's War achieved
Loss of Serbian land and refugees displaced in plan ill conceived
   KLA's power to attack Serbs was the essence,
   Stymied only by the Bolshevik's armed force presence,
Which proved the U. S. was the sole "organized terrorist group" as "weaved"

Citizen Hannin thought Clinton "blew it" by not considering all contingencies. With disgust he said, "Rhodes Scholar, my backside."

Another citizen, Millich, was aghast that the plight of "Serbian" refugees was totally ignored by the world, especially by some alleged "humanitarian" groups. He agonized that Kosovo, birthplace of Serbia, was turned over to Albanian immigrants who didn't even speak the language. As a foreboding precedent, the U. S. acted as judge, jury and executioner. She labeled the U. S. as an "economic blackmailer" of tiny countries who had no choice but to dance to its tune. She welcomed America to the "New World Disorder" brought about by Clinton's government.

Millich welcomed America to the "New World Disorder"
Brought on by Dictator Clinton's government—chief "discorder"
   "Gave" Kosovo to recent immigrants
   Who were Albanian rebel transplants,
And thereby destroyed Serbia's sovereign national border

One more citizen, Bozic, stated that the illegal NATO aggression on a sovereign nation "accidentally" murdered about 20,000 people in 78 days. Military, civilian, Chinese diplomats and Albanian Muslims were included in this "reverse ethnic cleansing" operation.

Brozic also observed that Clinton bragged about not losing a single man in combat, although two pilots were lost in Apache helicopter accidents.

Colhen's column informed readers that Europe's Balkan policy with its 15-nation bloc would provide $.5 billion annually over three years to

Kosovo, with or without Milosevic's presence in power. Serbia, however, would receive nothing as long as Milosevic remained in office. Democratic institutions had to be put in place and isolation of Milosevic appeared to be the thrusts of NATO's policy.

French officials said that real difficulties remained nevertheless, since Kosovo's financial institutions were impotent and unable to aid directly the Serbian people.

Schnieder described Clinton's "Third Way" war in Kosovo as the New World Order leader politics of "identifying with the moderate left," neither leftist, heavy-handed intervention nor not right, "laissez faire."

Senator Smith disagreed. The U. S. never had a vital national security interest in Kosovo. Military analyst, Collins, called U. S. interest in Kosovo "humanitarian" but not vital. The House of Representatives refused to endorse Clinton's War that had already been underway.

Although Clinton's air war brought Milosevic to the peace table and forced Serbia's troops to withdraw from Kosovo, critics pointed out its "shortcomings." Milosevic "completed " ethnic cleansing, he was still in power, Clinton "lucked out" and most Americans didn't view the outcome as a victory. The Chinese Embassy was bombed, Republicans never supported Clinton's War and U. S. ground troops would still be required indefinitely to "preserve the 'air strikes only' victory."

Russia decided to side with NATO not Serbia when talk of a possible NATO invasion force was bandied about. Yeltsin benefited with a major "independent" role for his troops in Kosovo and the likelihood of future aid.

Americans were relieved that Clinton's War was over. They did not feel triumphant, however. They felt that Clinton "lucked out" in Kosovo just as he did with impeachment.

Clinton's War in Kosovo was declared a "victory"
It sped up "ethnic cleansing," which was contradictory
    Our troops stationed indefinitely,
    "Foreign aid" to rise infinitely,

With U. S. "sell-out" arced on a one-world trajectory

Boudreaux and Finerman wrote of Yugoslavian police attempts to prevent frightened Serbian civilians from abandoning Kosovo. They refused to allow exhausted Serbs to pass or give them needed fuel.

Serbian troop withdrawal allowed Albanian rebels to attack viciously, loot and burn homes of Serbian civilians before NATO troops arrived. The spirit of KLA reprisals and "reverse ethnic cleansing" against Serbians was still alive. To fortify the plea, its leader, Pavic had moved from Belgrade to Pec in Kosovo. Serbs who remained in Kosovo minimized political damage to Milosevic, while Serbian Orthodox Christians pleaded with Serbian civilians to remain in Kosovo.

Yugoslavian troops would be permitted to recover military vehicles and equipment beyond the deadline because of fuel shortages. NATO troops would protect both Serbs and Albanians remaining in Kosovo in an impartial manner. In addition, the UN promised to "include Serbs in the government of Kosovo it will create."

Chapter 7

Serbian Troop Withdrawal from Kosovo, KFOR Occupation and Aftermath

After Serbia withdrew its troops from Kosovo, the aftermath evolved into Albanian "reverse ethnic cleansing" of the remaining Serbs and Gypsies from the Serbian province. The situation is described under the headings of Serbian Troops Withdraw from Kosovo and Reactions, Albanian "Ethnic Cleansing" of Gypsies from Kosovo, Slaughter of Serbians at Gracko, General Joseph Ralston Replaces General Wesley Clark as NATO Commander, Acrimony Continues between Serbs and Albanians in Kosovo, Four Months after NATO"s Occupation of Kosovo and "Peaceful Coexistence" Continues in Kosovo since NATO's Occupation.

Serbian Troop Withdraw from Kosovo and Reactions

Forty thousand Serbian troops completed their withdrawal from Kosovo on June 20, 1999 reported Myers. Serbian control over the province, which is the religious, cultural and historical birthplace of Serbia, officially ended. NATO's Secretary General Solana officially announced the formal end of the 78-day air strike devastation of Serbia.

Increased numbers of a peacekeeping KFOR continued relentlessly to invade Kosovo.

Kosovo's Albanian Muslims were elated and some KLA members sought retribution against Serbian Christian civilians by burning and looting a dozen of their homes despite the presence of 18,000 NATO troops. The rebels and NATO were waiting for formal signing of an accord to demilitarize the KLA.

Italian forces discovered a KLA arsenal of mortar rounds, land mines, anti-tank rockets and shoulder-fired missiles. British troops disarmed two rebel patrols. U. S. Marines arrested a rebel sniper who was accused of killing three Serbians.

Citizens Davidio and Sharp expressed their views regarding Clinton's claim to victory in Kosovo.

Davidio claimed that the U. S. and NATO won the Kosovo War
Cost $100 "mill" per day to end this 78-day meddling chore
    Milosevic still ruled his tiny nation,
    Serbia ruined by air strike devastation,
And "Wily Willie" spouted his stale propaganda we all abhor

Clinton's air strikes on Kosovo caused Albanian Muslims to flee
It accelerated "ethnic cleansing" at a breathless pace you see
    Now the cost of re-building would escalate,
    U. S. troops deployed to an "open end" date
With Milosevic the real victor, in power and joyous with glee

Citizen Sharp opined that Russia's seizure of Pristina's airport might yet prove disastrous for Clinton. He called the war a one-sided conflict with only one-sided aggression. It appeared that the "victory" would be shared with Russia much like its late entry during the last few weeks of hostilities in W. W. II. He viewed the Kosovo operation as a communist success story. Milosevic was clearly the winner.

Cohen's column revealed that the G-7 nations' relief plan and political support for the Balkans required Yugoslavia to institute "democratic and economic reforms." Among its provisions were that "Milosevic must depart and no aid would be extended to Serbia."

Unsurprisingly, Clinton wanted a meeting with G-7 and Balkan leaders to draw the Balkans into the West and expand Western Europe's Mini One World scheme.

The KLA exacted a pledge from NATO to "duly consider" allowing it to form a provisional army akin to the National Guard in the U. S. Further details were unavailable at the time. The pledge would permit the KLA to continue as a military and political force in Kosovo. Meanwhile, the KLA agreed to a "cease fire and gradual demilitarization."

Consideration of a rebel "National Guard" met with anger and opposition by Yugoslavia and Germany. Albright told the Fatherland that an agreement could not be reached without its inclusion.

Clinton touted Slovenia as a "questionable" paradigm possibility when it defied Milosevic's ethnic cleansing. Slovenia declared independence from Yugoslavia in June 1991, withstood a "bloodless" war and was now free and prosperous.

At the time, however, Slovenia contained only two percent Serbs with 98 percent Roman Catholics among its 2 million inhabitants. Slovenia wanted to join the European Union and was working toward that end while it actively sought membership in NATO.

In pure Clintonian fashion, he "spin-doctored" and re-named the Balkan countries as "Southeastern Europe" in a revisionist attempt to eliminate the negative connotations of "Balkan stigma and Balkanization."

Clinton still desired a submissive "democratic" leader in Serbia, especially one who would "knuckle under and submit to international meddling in international affairs under any pretext."

Polloshka, city official, had about 100 Albanian bodies exhumed from mass graves in Kjakovica, and re-interred in the municipal cemetery wrote Kifner. The names of the dead were not available.

Enda's column described Clinton's subdued manner as he comforted refugees at Skope, Kosovo. Conveniently forgetting the "collateral damage" inflicted by the air strikes he had ordered. "I feel your pain" Clinton took pains to caution the civilians about land mines and the damage the deadly explosives might inflict! Clinton wanted them to be patient until they could return safely to their homes. Some refugees returned to Kosovo but soon departed dejected because "there were no homes." Many refugees cheered the president and would not forget the gift of freedom he'd brought.

Clinton also told peacekeepers they must now "secure the place and protect Albanian and Serbs alike." "The U. S. would not stand for 'ethnic cleansing and genocide by either side,'" he said; apparently with swollen tongue in cheek?

British foreign Secretary Cook and other European foreign ministers toured Velika Krusa where 105 people were massacred penned Vrazo. They reviewed skeletal remains and expressed deep shock. The group felt the war was justified and hoped to see Kosovo as a "peaceful, multiethnic and multireligious society."

The Serbian Orthodox Church complained of Albanian "ethnic cleansing" attacks on Serbs. Meanwhile, 50,000 to 120,000 Serbs in Kosovo had fled to Serbia and Montenegro. Many Serbs were too scared to return despite "assurances from peacekeepers."

Serbs fired on a Marine checkpoint at Zegra reported Myers. The Marines killed one Serb and wounded three others. Zegra is a hotbed for violence between Serbs and the KLA.

Many Serbs fled from Zegra in fear, even though Orthodox Church leaders pleaded with them to stay wrote Myers. At least a dozen Serbian homes were seen in flames.

After the Serbs fled, Albanians were seen going from house-to-house retrieving whatever was left behind. Some Albanians sought revenge and others retrieved "what was their own." U. S. Marines "just watched and did nothing to halt the exodus or the Albanians from looting."

NATO commander, General Clark, called for an international police force to quell the deaths and violence caused by returning Albanians seeking revenge against Serbs remaining in Kosovo. Sixteen civilian deaths were reported in the last day and a half, June 24-25, 1999. An international police force of 3,000 was planned to take over protection from criminal activity.

Clinton expressed concern abut the turbulent situation, but was "not particularly surprised after what they've been through." Lieutenant General Jackson promised "to protect all citizens equally." More NATO forces were coming in every day and everyone would be safer.

Schellenberg, NATO housing coordinator, surveyed housing damage in Kosovo. Between 30—40 percent of the houses were estimated to be uninhabitable. He charged the Serbs with systematic destruction after the bombing commenced. Schellenberg noted exceptions like schools and apartment buildings, presumably owned by influential Serbs, had been excluded from destruction.

Clinton wanted to remove Milosevic from office in the worst way and was doing everything he could to accomplish that aim wrote McManus. Clinton was intent on transforming Yuglslavia into a more democratic country.

Clinton wanted to "evict" Milosevic, the "ethnic cleansing" clod
Ordered the CIA: "disrupt" Slobo's financial dealings abroad
   "Computer hack" into each one of his accounts,
   "Drain" funds from foreign banks in any amounts,
And "give" political aid to democratic forces as a prod

Adamant Clinton and European allies vowed not to furnish reconstruction money to Serbia until Milosevic was ousted. Clinton banked on a frustrated and disappointed Serbian public to rise up against Milosevic.

He wanted to legitimize "computer hacking" to ruin financially Milosevic and his backers. Clinton encouraged Serbia's military leaders to "turncoat and quisling" on Miloseic. He even hinted that military leaders who became "quislings" might be spared prosecution for war crimes. In addition, Clinton offered a $5 million reward for the "arrest and conviction of Milosevic, but not to kill him."

KLA's rebel leader Thaci and others supplied information regarding targets to NATO during the bombing wrote Myers. Now, NATO made the KLA partners in re-building Kosovo. After KLA's disarmament, it would be converted into a "civilian police force and/or a provisional army a la the U. S. National Guard."

Haxhijai, former rebel, claimed this was not just a war against the Serbs, but also a struggle for leadership in the KLA; hence, assassinations purged leaders at the top echelons. The charge of assassinations, arrests and purges of rivals at the top were made by former rebel commanders and some Western diplomats.

Fisher related that Germany's Brigadier General Von Korff imposed a curfew from midnight to 5:a.m. on the city of Prizren to stifle Albanian revenge and "reverse ethnic cleansing." He wanted to prevent more slayings, car thefts, looting and burning of homes. Fourteen Serbs were slain in Pristina.

Czech president, Havel, condemned the revenge of Albanians and said, "They must live in peace with the Serb minority so they have no reason to flee." Thus far, return of the Albanian refugees had not been peaceful. The village of Belo Polje was burned and looted by Albanians pushing wheelbarrows. The KLA tortured gypsies. Thousands of Serbs had fled Pec. Some Albanians acknowledged the ethnic cleansing charge and said, "They were simply practicing the golden rule."

Impe of Jack Van Impe Ministries, on his television program, revealed that Clinton 's War cost $3 billion in bombing expenses, $5 billion to rebuild infrastructure and $2 billion annually to maintain peace in Kosovo.

He added that the long-range intent of globalists was to incorporate all European nations, including former Russian states into NATO and expand its hegemony to Africa and the Far East.

Impe also remarked that several thousand Serbs in Kosovo had been killed "before" they retaliated with "ethnic cleansing" against the Albanian rebels. This revelation was barely mentioned in the media.

Harden described the first major anti-government demonstration in Cacak where a crowd of 20,000 demanded Milosevic's removal. Cacak is a city where the opposition party in Serbia ran the government.

Milosevic was accused of bringing shame on Serbia in the eyes of the world, committing robbery and murder in Kosovo, covering up failure by a campaign of lies on state-owned media and provoking attacks from our traditional Western allies. Some protesters urged Milosevic to go to Cuba and study Stalinism there.

Up to 25 rallies against Milosevic were planned throughout Serbia, eventually culminating in the biggest demonstration at Belgrade.

The International Criminal Tribunal (ICT) would only make a thorough inquiry at a handful of shoddy graves filled with slaughtered Albanians wrote Fisher. There were just too many graves to be examined with available personnel. Survivors wanted them to come, make an official record, conduct autopsies and allow surviving families to bury properly their dead. "Without the inquiry into every grave, it loses all credibility," remarked one KLA official.

The ICT was focused on gathering evidence to try and convict Milosevic and plans were made to concentrate on seven massacre sites. The evidence gathered consisted of exhumation, identification, photographs and witnesses.

General Clark said that Milosevic was gathering intelligence and sending reinforcements into Montenegro reported Schmitt. The moves were designed to place Serbs into a position of authority against Djukanovic who is pro Western and seeking its aid and support. (It appeared that NATO's non-response was a veiled threat to "intervene or invade" if Milosevic attempted to oust Djukanovic. Invasion would be congruent with overall Clinton-NATO international, militant meddling, and one world policy in the conspicuous absence of U. S. national security interests.)

General Clark accused Milosevic of conducting a "soft" campaign to expel Albanians from the Sanjak region between Serbia and Montenegro. The soon-to-be 55,000 NATO force would be available for "peace-keeping" should this situation escalate.

About 10,000 Serbs in Novi Sad demonstrated against Milosevic and threatened to "throw him out" if he didn't resign scribed Harden. The demonstrators blamed their troubles on Milosevic. Novi Sad is the capital of Voivodina, which is the largest food-producing province. The province consists of one million Serbs and one million Hungarian, Croats, Slovaks and Romanians.

> For its ills, Novi Sad protesters blamed Milosevic in defiance
> For ended lost wars, ruined Serb's economy and destroyed self reliance
>> Crops not harvested 'cause fuel was short,
>> Jobs were lost, bridge repairs he did abort,
> Vowed to "throw their leader out" even it took some degree of violence

Thousands of Albanian Muslims were celebrating the anniversary of their "unilaterally" declared independence from Serbian rule according to Price. British paratroopers fired on a carload of Albanian revelers, killing two and wounding two others. British soldiers standing guard in front of a building believed their lives were in danger when a white car drove past them as an automatic rifle was fired.

Witnesses blamed the revelers who had already driven past the building twice and fired into the air as bystanders cheered. Three British soldiers fired at the car as it made its third pass.

British officials said the shooting was under investigation. Lieutenant Commander Howells said, "That the occasion was just a happy celebration was mythical. Serbs were intimidated, shot and beaten up."

Russian officials were miffed at NATO's refusal to "permit" Russia to send more peace keepers to Kosovo. Russia 's role had to be resolved before more troops were allowed and they did not want its troops to serve under NATO's command.

At the same time, NATO members, Hungary, Romania and Bulgaria refused to allow Russian air transports to enter their air space. Simultaneously, gypsies were fleeing Rodesh for Montenegro to escape revengeful Albanians.

Spielmann described the final deal negotiated between NATO and Russian troops in Kosovo. Russia would send 3,600 troops and 16 liaison officers, have flexibility in defining their mission and assign Russian officers at all levels of the NATO command.

They would patrol a sector controlled by U. S., German and French forces. A Russian would be commander of Pristina's airport with 750 Russian troops stationed in the vicinity.

Citizen Bozic accused Clinton of spin doctoring and trying to justify Clinton's War by touting Slovenia as the model state that challenged Milosevic. He related that neither Milosevic nor Serbs cared about Slovenia because it was a "pure Slovenian population." The was no interest in halting its secession in 1991 because "there were no Serbs there to protect."

Bozic reminded readers that Kosovo had ancient Serbian roots and is the birthplace of Serbian Orthodox Christianity, culture, folklore and civilization as a sovereign country. In Kosovo, inundation by an "illegal" immigrant population that suffused into a majority did not constitute a right to steal and take away a nation's sovereignty.

An Associated Press release noted that 350 Kosovar burials were suspected near Ljubenic. If confirmed, it might be viewed as the largest ethnic cleansing burial ground in Kosovo.

Meanwhile, city officials from Nis and Sombor called for Milosevic's resignation. A petition drive for Milosevic's "heave ho" started in Belgrade and was expected to cover the entire country.

Secretary of Defense Cohen "warned" other nations not to give the indicted war criminal refuge—without further explanation.

Albanian "Ethnic Cleansing" of the Gypsies

Reitman scribed that Gypsies or Roma in Kosovo were being driven from their homes by returning Albanian refugees for "collaborating with Serbs." Majority Albanians "ethnically cleansed" minority Gypsies even though they constituted a very small percentage of the population.

The Gypsies appealed to the UN to send them to other nations, but the plea was rejected as "unrealistic." Besides, "other nations didn't want them." The United Nations preferred Gypsies remain in Kosovo "in security and dignity. This is their country and their home."

Hasani, a Roma, contended that the Albanians wanted an "ethnically pure" Kosovo and "you cannot kill a Gypsy for alleged looting like stealing a TV." Another Roma, Beriska, said, "The Albanians were taking revenge on innocent people."

Some Gypsies who fled with Albanian refugees feared returning home because "they will kill us." Hasani said, "Going abroad is the only hope for Gypsies."

According to war crimes investigators, estimates of at least 10,000 Albanian Muslims were slain by Serbs reported Kifner. More and more gravesites were discovered according to Williamson, a legal officer and investigator. He opined, "The exact number of victims may never by known."

The Hague Tribunal had recorded 280 gravesites and 6,100 bodies to date. Many Albanians were disinterring corpses and giving them a proper burial.

More than 1,000 Serb army reservists blocked roads near Kracujevac demanding back pay immediately as per an anonymous news item. They also demanded political changes. General Perisic, former Army Chief of Staff, was ready to join the reservists. He favored political removal of the present leadership in Serbia.

Slaughter of Serbians at Gracko

An Associated Press news item reported that NATO peacekeepers found 14 Serbs dead on a farm road, worst single act of violence to date. Peacekeepers had been hard pressed to prevent attacks by Albanians on Serbs. It was believed the Albanian Muslims were engaged in "reverse ethnic cleansing" attacks.

Reitman and Glover wrote that NATO troops were searching for the killers of 24 Serbs found on a wheat farm near Gracko. Lieutenant General Jackson regretted the deaths and said his troops "can't be everywhere at once." His priority was to confiscate large supplies of arms from homes and cars in Kosovo. At the time, arms were legal in Kosovo. General Jackson was unaware of how many arms the KLA had.

Gracko residents accused KFOR of "ignoring" pleas for greater security and made calls that requested aid when the wheat farmers failed to return home. They also reported other Serb residents had turned up "missing." Serbs feared KLA members as terrorists because they were allied with KFOR. Most of Gracko's villagers said they would remain because there was "no other place to go."

Upwards of 40 percent or 80,000 Serbs have departed Kosovo since the arrival of NATO's KFOR wrote Hedges. The exodus was likely to continue inasmuch as KFOR seemed "powerless and/or unwilling to halt reciprocal ethnic cleansing."

NATO officials promised to apprehend the killers responsible for the massacre in Gracko. The village of Gracko had been a sitting duck for assault since Albanian Muslims populated the surrounding area. KLA leaders denied participation in the massacre and asked Serbs to remain in Kosovo.

KFOR had thus far detained several hundred Albanians for murder, arson and looting against Serbs and their property.

Belgrade requested the UN Security Council stop the violence and allow Serbian forces back into Kosovo to protect Serbs but the request was denied reported an anonymous Associated Press item. Lieutenant General Jackson understood the Albanian motive for revenge but would not tolerate it under any circumstance.

An unsigned news item related that NSC advisor Berger pledged $500 million in relief aid to Kosovo in a speech before the Council of Foreign Relations in Brussels. The U. S. would lead relief efforts for food, housing, health care, sanitation, land mine clearance, human rights programs, police force installation and aid to refugees in Albania and Macedonia.

NATO's Successor, General Joseph Ralston Replaces General Wesley Clark

General Joseph Ralston was Clinton's choice to succeed General Wesley Clark as NATO's top commander next year as per an anonymous Associated Press blurb. Senate ratification was required. General Ralston was passed over for the Chief of Staff job when he retreated from consideration because an old adulterous "affair" threatened to embarrass both him and the Pentagon. His selection was perhaps a reward for his loyalty, especially to Defense Secretary Cohen. (Wasn't it strange that alleged adulterous episodes involving Clinton and Paula, Kathleen, Juanita, Monica et al. didn't hinder his assignment and responsibility as Commander in Chief of U. S. Armed Forces, CINC?)

Allard, Georgetown University professor, observed that selection of an Air Force General was in keeping with the "evolution of NATO from a ground army to an air power and a reflection of changing times"—a la Kosovo.

General Ralston is described as a low-key, efficient, day-to-day functionary, second in charge behind the Joint Chiefs of Staff. Defense Secretary Cohen trusted Ralston, who served as a "shuttle diplomat" to India and Pakistan and among national security agencies. On occasion, he had "stood in" for General Shelton, Joint Chiefs Chairman.

It seemed strangely conspicuous that the article did not discuss General Clark's contributions to victory in Clinton's Air War over Serbia or the reasons for his removal. To be sure, media evidence periodically alluded to "White House dissatisfaction with his independence, loyalty and lack of blind adherence to Clinton's policy." It appeared General Clark was not a "complete White House team player."

An anonymous Associated Press squib news item reported that the U. S. would compensate the families of three Chines reporters killed and 27 persons injured in the bombing of the Chinese Embassy. As is usual in such matters, "reparations are voluntary without an admission of guilt." Beijing would decide on distribution of the pay off.

The Chinese government still refused to accept "faulty intelligence" as the reason for the fatal mistake. It demanded compensation, an inquiry and punishment for those responsible.

An anonymous news item related that British Prime Minster Blair made a "triumphant" visit to Pristina urging Albanians to coexist peacefully with Serbians. He told the people that NATO "intervened" to bring peace and justice to Kosovo and not allow Kosovar Serbs to be oppressed.

Blair was in Pristina to visit British troops after attending a summit in Sarajevo where 50 nations agreed to a "Balkan Stability Pact." The pact allowed assistance to all Balkan nations—except Serbia, which was singled out for "non-humanitarian" punishment. (Ostensibly, Serbia would be excluded from assistance until Milosevic was ousted and democratic reforms introduced.)

Serbia promptly dismissed the pact as a "cover for Western exploitation." Serbia boldly asserted it "would reconstruct its country through trade—not aid."

Borba, a pro government newspaper, labeled the summit a "tragic-comical gathering of powerful Western nations and their Balkan bootlickers."

Following Blair's visit, a large explosion damaged a Serbian Orthodox Church then under construction. No casualties were reported. The church was not an historical religious site or place of worship, but more of a symbol to Serbian rule

Acrimony Continues between Albanians and Serbians in Kosovo

Hatred between Serbs and Albanians continued to seethe after a bombing damaged a Serbian Orthodox Church noted an Associated Press news item. Serbs doubted KFOR's ability to restrain Albanians. Farmer Savic, said, "All we see is KFOR cooperating with Albanians" and "The peace keepers don't have enough troops."

The Albanians were rather distrustful of Russian troops since they have had traditional close bonds with Serbia.

Major Farrell, KFOR Operations Officer, stated, "We're trying to protect both sides, but the hatred is so deep."

Attacks by Albanians continued in Kosovo according to a Knight-Ridder news item. Fewer than 80,000 Serbs remained in Kosovo and more were exiting the province each day. Even with KFOR's presence, dozens of Serbs had been killed, many more kidnapped and hundreds threatened and ejected from their homes. One woman, Ljubica Vujovic, was found drowned in her bathtub fully clothed, probably murdered for shock value and her two-bedroom apartment!

An anonymous New York Times news blurb described continued threats and attacks on Russian peacekeepers. Albanians threatened and fired upon Russian troops who were protecting Serbs remaining in Kosovo and guarding several checkpoints.

Citizen Queenan was upset at Clinton's "stupid, short-sighted policy" of intentionally giving away NATO's battle plans. The blunder assured the Serbs that ground forces would not be used. It incited the Serbs to "massacre and ethnic cleanse" Albanians in Kosovo. Sadly, it could have been avoided.

Another citizen, Ezz, viewed the UN's implementation in Kosovo as a denial of independence for Albanian self-rule and lack of justice by allowing war criminals to flee to Serbia. Under those circumstances, Ezz wasn't surprised the Albanians turned to violence.

Glover described how the Albanian crime pattern pointed to "reverse ethnic cleansing" against the remaining Serbs in Kosovo. In Pristina, Serbs were intimidated, letter warnings mailed to leave their homes, personal and physical assaults threatened and murder promised.

It was reported that the military police had dozens of Serbs slain by shots to the head after being bound hand and foot. Villages were burned and villagers slain as threats and acts of violence continued.

Bishop Artemije, Serbian Orthodox Church, said it was organized activity. Forty churches had been vandalized and burned. He blamed NATO and the UN for the organized acts of terrorism. He added, "KLA's Thaci had the power to stop 'reverse ethnic cleansing' if he chose."

Pristina's Serbian population was down from 27,000 inhabitants to somewhat less than 2,000. Those Serbs that remained were mainly the elderly, disabled and without families.

Kissinger, dedicated one world proponent, was "puzzled" at Europe's 15 leaders who desired to create a separate military force, capable of acting without approval from both the U. S. and NATO. The leaders desired "autonomy and freedom from dominance" by the U. S. and NATO.

Kissinger, of course, was aghast and against any notion of "sovereignty and nationalism." He touted NATO because "its motives were pure and was the only posse in town?" He also argued, "Humanitarian and national interest distinctions vanish when 'narrowly defined.'"

Briefly, Kissinger wanted to expand NATO's humanitarian right to intervene and traverse sovereign borders without autonomous and rebellious resistance over cries for independence and narrow nationalism from its members. Ironically, Clinton's War was fought in Kosovo to "impose autonomy and independence for rebellious Albanians" in sovereign Serbia.

The UN deployed 30 international police to "granny patrol" Pristina's streets after many elderly Serbian women were murdered wrote Rozen. Albanians unabashedly and callously coveted their apartments.

Only 20 percent of the original 27,000 Serbian residents, mostly elderly, remained in Pristina. Most Serbs stayed in their domiciles and were afraid to leave their apartments.

A massive rally was staged by Milosevic's opponents demanding his ouster scribed Erlanger. The rally was hardly unified because many divisions existed among opposition leaders, a circumstance beneficial to Milosevic.

A new election and Milosevic's ouster or resignation was favored. Whatever, Milosevic's term of office expires in July 2001 and he didn't intend to resign prematurely.

NATO's Dutch troops ordered Serbs to turn in their weapons or face arrest reported an Associated Press news item. Serbian police had given weapons to its civilians. After the warning, 120 weapons had been turned in shortly thereafter.

Albanian politician, Rugova, referred to Kosovo as the "Republic of Kosovo." Meanwhile, Milosevic's rivals called for his ouster because he had "plunged the country into four disastrous wars and left it in economic ruin."

Gall's column scribed that "peaceful coexistence" of Serbs and Albanians was failing and "de facto" segregation and resettlement of Serbs into enclaves or ghettos had to be considered. The U. S. and friends opposed partitioning Kosovo into Albanian Muslim and Serbian Orthodox Christian enclaves because "it abandoned the goals of its air strikes." Clinton and Albright would have had to admit defeat and they would have none of that.

The U. S. and NATO were "determined" to protect Serbs even if it had to guard individual homes and apartments. UN's Kouchner left a "Clinton out" for temporary or provisional resettlement, i. e., if security couldn't be ensured. As of August 26, 1999, peacekeepers had failed to halt Albanian violence or protect Serbs and Gypsies.

Milosevic wanted Kosovo to be partitioned with the north occupied by Serbs and the south by Albanians. The U. S. and its allies nixed the notion.

Serbs accused the UN and NATO of violating the peace agreement, which promised to protect Serbs wrote Watson and Martelle. They were angry at almost daily attacks on Serbs in Kosovo, so much so that Serbs threatened to re-enter Kosovo.

General Pavkovic said the KLA was not disarmed or dismantled, Yugoslavian sovereignty ignored and UN poised to issue new passports and Customs' rules for Kosovo. They also didn't protect the borders, create a political solution for Kosovo or provide security for non-Albanians. A plan to fashion an Albanian force of 3,000 rebels carrying weapons as an "honor guard" was in the works. To Serbia, this meant the "honor guard" could constitute the core of an Albanian Army potentially useful in its fight for eventual independence.

Avdeyev, deputy foreign minister, was of the opinion that "separating Kosovo from Yugoslavia was a spin-doctored euphemism for preserving territorial integrity." General Pavkovic said Serbian patience was being exhausted because Kosovo's Serbs were endangered daily, Serbian sovereignty was moot and the KLA was getting clear support. He was not fearful of KFOR, except its air power.

Some skirmishes had occurred between Albanians and Serbs and between Albanians and French soldiers. Some Serb paramilitary units had moved into the divided city of Kosovska Mitrovica. French General Thomann said he had no authority from stopping people from moving about and no border existed between Serbia and Kosovo.

After three months of "peace," only 97,000 Serbs remained in Kosovo amid daily assaults by Albanians and more Serbs continued to exit out of fear and prospects of a dismal future in Kosovo.

General Pavkovic remarked that his 3rd Army losses from air strikes were minimal. They lost 462 dead, 13 tanks, six armored personal carriers, three artillery pieces, nine anti aircraft guns and 10 vehicles, and the police lost 114 officers. His revelations contradicted NATO's claim that air strikes inflicted heavy losses on the military. Besides, few remnants of Serb's heavy weapons were ever discovered by KFOR.

Citizen Bozic deduced that ongoing Albanian attacks on Serbians exemplified their real objective, which was to "ethnically cleanse" all Serbs from Kosovo. When that feat was accomplished, there'd be no further need for "peace keepers" to protect Albanian civilians.

Bozic wrote that NATO helped the KLA kill Serbian civilians not only in Kosovo but also throughout Yugoslavia. He reasoned that when the KLA no longer needed NATO's assistance, they would attack their "bene-factor-nurturer-accomplice."

He also recalled the Albanians began their ambush attacks on Serbs in 1989 and every "able" Albanian was a member of the KLA.

A plan to transform a demilitarized KLA into a 5,000-member civilian "Kosovo Corps" was postponed for two days according to an Associated Press news item. The KLA wanted this force to become the basis of an Albanian Army in an "independent" Kosovo. The KLA also desired to retain more weapons and control the "Kosovo Corps."

NATO objected to KLA claims and insisted that peace keepers must be the only armed force in Kosovo.

Russia and Serbia opposed any plan that maintained the Kosovo Liberation Army under the alias, "Kosovo Corps."

NATO announced that the KLA had already turned in 10,000 weapons and that "demilitarization was effectively complete," despite evidence to the contrary.

An Associated Press news item reported that 40,000 people protested in downtown Belgrade demanding Milosevic's resignation. Although the number of Alliance for Democratic Change protesters was estimated at 40,000, the figure was lower than expected.

Father Janic declared the Albanians wanted to destroy every vestige and reminder of Serbian culture to prevent their return. He said the destruction was organized and not the "work of villagers." He didn't think KFOR could halt the destruction without assistance from the KLA.

Riot police swinging batons beat down anti-government protesters related the Associated Press. The protesters, led by Djindjic and Protic, said they planned to demonstrate in front of government buildings in New Belgrade but were beaten back. They said their numbers were growing and planned to march against Milosevic's residence.

Protesters demanded Milosevic's ouster and democratic changes. In all, 40, 000 protesters marched in Belgrade, 20,000 in Novi Sad and 10,000 in Nis. They charged the government with "creating an atmosphere of fear." The government counter-charged the protest leaders with "hiring criminals to provoke clashes."

Four Months after NATO's Occupation Began

After four months of "occupation" in Kosovo, NATO has been unable to achieve the unrealistic goal of a "multiethnic integrated society" wrote Martelle. Instead, "ghettoization" is de facto and peacekeepers enforce estranged divisions between Serbs and Albanians, both groups seething with fear and hatred.

Another goal, halting the persecution of Albanians, was made a mockery since Serbian paramilitary groups and security police had terrorized Albanians and left 11,000 dead and 100,000 homes badly damaged or destroyed.

Serbs remaining in Kosovo had formed defiant enclaves surrounded by revengeful Albanians who feel "Serbs have no place here anymore." In effect, two armed camps engage in frequent clashes and fear permeates the air.

A UN report estimated that fewer that half of the original 200,000 Serbs in Kosovo remained.

An anonymous news item related that "selective humanitarian" Clinton opposed a European plan to provide heating oil, kindling wood and other assistance to Yugoslavians in order to cope with the coming winter. The

$5 million in heating oil would help them adjust to oil shortages caused by NATO's bombings of its refineries.

Clinton feared the aid would buttress Milosevic's intransigence and discourage protests and attempts to oust him from office. European allies did not agree. They rejected Clinton's brand of "isolationism" as the only way to remove Milosevic.

General Reinhardt, German commander of KFOR in Pristina, was furious when 1,500 Albanians attacked a NATO-protected convoy of four busses and many cars loaded with 155 Serbs leaving for Montenegro. Twenty Serbian civilian cars became separated near Pec and were attacked. Italian police had to rescue them. General Reinhardt said he took undisclosed actions against the officers responsible.

General Reinhardt was dismayed at the lack of tolerance displayed by Albanians since the Serbs along with their possessions were leaving Kosovo. A change in their mental processes was needed. He promised his troops would do everything possible to protect Serbs and appealed for them to stay and/or return to Kosovo. His main goal was to "build trust" between Serbs and Albanians

"Slick's" potent weapon for "peddling meddling" is ethnic immigrant suffusion
　"Illegal lawbreakers" are most acceptable, which adds to the confusion
　　A ploy for denationalization,
　　"De facto" partition of each nation
That grants rebels autonomy; falsely "preserves" sovereignty's illusion

Blair and Chirac denied they were "intruding" on NATO's territory; rather, the plan would establish a capability in circumstances not appropriate for NATO. They also finally admitted that the "U. S. shouldered 80 percent of the air strikes and moved most of the heavy military equipment during Clinton's War."

British Defense Secretary Hoon noted that, despite enormous "paper" troop strength, NATO nations had difficulty assembling the tens of thousands of troops necessary for invading Kosovo. The reality was that only two percent of the combined European forces were actually available for deployment!

Clinton, clad in a wind breaker jacket with the CINC logo visible on the right side, visited the troops at several locations. He shared Thanksgiving dinner with them, posed for pictures with soldiers, crowed about the successful war without combat casualties and thanked them for "reversing Serbian ethnic cleansing." He also remarked that they had a "chance, not a guarantee," to build a lasting peace in Kosovo.

Clinton worked the barracks like a polished entertainer in a lounge act and chatted freely with the soldiers akin to seeking votes while on the campaign trail. After the visits with troops, he departed for Italy to return home from his 45th foreign trip.

According to the Associated Press, Britain and France pushed for a new 50,000 to 60,000 "independent" European Union military force capable of full deployment with 60 days. The idea was to decrease Europe" dependence on the U. S. Blair and Chirac would urge leaders of the 15-nation European Union at the next meeting in Helsinki to agree to furnish necessary troops, ships, aircraft and armament to implement the new force. They hoped to establish the force within a year.

Britain's Conservative Party denounced the plan as dangerous and a threat to NATO's stability. Blair was accused of yielding to an anti-American stance led by Chirac's influence.

While on a ten-day visit to European nations, Clinton made the pre-dictable public relations' "photo op" treks to Kosovo to bask in the success of "his war." He crowed about destroying much of Serbia's infrastructure, denationalizing a part of Serbia, establishing an autonomous Albanian Kosovo and implementing his "mini Western one-world objective." He urged Albanian Kosovars to "forgive the Serbs and re-shape a new Kosovo."

Many Albanians cheered wildly, although many found it difficult to forgive. Clinton urged them to try anyway.

KFOR experienced difficulty in "imposing" peace. About 1,700 police struggled to control high crime rates, obedience to traffic laws and establishing the rudiments of a civil society.

Citizen Bozic had some choice thoughts on Clinton's visit to Kosovo over the Thanksgiving holiday period in 1999. He thought the Serbs had little to be thankful for due to Clinton's War.

Citizen Bozic wrote that Clinton visited Kosovo, site of devastation
Where 22 thousand Serb civilians were "killed by air strikes" in this tiny Slav nation
    Most manufacturing firms "wasted,"
    Hospitals and schools " missile pasted,"
Like a murderer who returned to the crime scene of vast, obscene obliteration

Bozic wrote Clinton gained nothing by the merciless bombing missions
Just more instability, ingrained hatred and ethnic suspicions
    Gave "Albs" the "green light" for ethnic cleanse,
    Through Serb's withdrawal permissive lens,
Though he "begged" them, "Cease the daily home burning and killing commissions"

Citizen Ross opined that Clinton's "photo op presence," in an otherwise fabulous photo of beaming soldiers' faces in Kosovo featured in the newspaper, was an "unfortunate blemish."

Ruddy, editor of Vortex, wrote "Clinton went into Kosovo for one reason only—to distract attention from Juanita Broaddrick's alleged rape charge and save his political hide!" He further wrote that Clinton placed American lives at risk in an illegal, undeclared war of no strategic importance to our national security and wreaked "collateral damage" on innocent civilians—especially women and children. He further charged that Clinton's War cost American taxpayers billions of dollars to wreck Serbia. Of course U. S. taxpayer costs would continue to escalate in order to re-build the province Kosovo, but not elsewhere in Serbia.

In addition, polls suggested that the attack on Serbia was a diversion from China's alleged theft of nuclear secrets and White House cover-ups. Poll results also indicated that possible loss of American lives was not worth Clinton's War for peace.

Other critics of Clinton's War in Kosovo alleged that "Slick" began the air strikes to remove the adverse effects of his sordid affair with Monica Lewinsky and the negative impression of impeachment proceedings from newspaper headlines, magazine articles and television coverage.

Citizen Legg charged the Civil War in Kosovo commenced by KLA separatists bent on "separation from Serbia."

Jack Impe of television's Impe Ministries contended that several thousands of Serbs were killed "before" the Serbs retaliated with their brand of "ethnic cleansing"

Citizen Larsen also found the same photo of the infamous draft dodger Clinton smiling amidst so many soldiers stationed in Kosovo that had sworn to give their lives for their country "so disturbing." Larsen opined that any attempt to explain the photo would probably have been misunderstood.

A Serbian court sentenced Dr. Flora Brovina, pediatrician and poet, to 12 years in prison for committing terrorism during U. S.—NATO air strikes in Kosovo. She led the Albanian League of Women and was charged with "aiding the separatist guerrilla movement (KLA) fighting Serbian forces. She participated in activities for the KLA during the bombings. Another charge filed against Dr. Flora Brovina was her "wanting to change borders and unite Kosovo with Albania."

Dr. Brovina defended herself by describing her actions as "purely humanitarian, helping women and children and attempting to elevate health standards." She claimed involvement in anti-war activities including peace marches."

According to the Associated Press, China and the U. S. agreed on "just" compensation for the "mistaken" U. S.—NATO bombing of China's Embassy in Belgrade and Chinese protester's well-orchestrated damage to an U. S. Embassy and consulates in China.

The U. S. would seek $28 million from Congress to liquidate its obligation to China, while China would pay $2.87 million for damages inflicted by angry Chinese demonstrators on the embassy and consular offices according to Andrews, State Department legal adviser. Andrews was hopeful that the settlement would indicate a "more positive trend between capitalist America and Communist China!

It seemed strange that the State Department didn't mention "just" compensation for thousands of innocent Serbian civilians killed and wounded as a result of mistaken "collateral damage" bombing!

Two Albanian gunmen killed one Serb and wounded eight others by spraying automatic gunfire on a café in Drahovac wrote the Associated Press. The lone Serb killed was the café owner. Peacekeepers "rushed" to the scene but the two gunmen had escaped.

Over 100 angry Serbs gathered in the Town Square and demanded that "peacekeepers" stop treating the Albanian criminals as "your allies."

Citizen Knudson noticed that "Clinton urged Kosovars to forgive the Serbs for their purges of Kosovo's Albanians." (Yet simultaneously, hypocritical Clinton refused to forgive Republicans who conducted the impeachment trial. Reports indicate that he's still bent on a political vendetta to destroy the managers.)

Knudson ended his comments when he recalled bitingly that "monarch Clinton was above the law."

Schlafly reported ominously that Berger pledged more "interventions" and that the only acceptable position for the world's most powerful nations were to support these missions. "America must respond to local conflicts, i. e., just the ones the 'internationalists' choose." One world zealot Berger uttered the comments at a Bilderberg Steering Committee meeting held at the Library of Congress on November 4, 1999.

He urged his listeners to "defend our (internationalist) beliefs together when they are threatened." Berger also labeled foes of Clinton's agenda as a "dominant minority" who's efforts against international spending were likely to fail."

Schlafly, citing other sources, wrote the Clinton administration lied to the American people about the magnitude of atrocities to justify Clinton's air strikes. Cohen claimed 100,000 dead and the State Department asserted that up to 500,000 were feared killed. But, the UN War Crimes investigators found only 2,108 bodies. Spanish pathologist, Pujol, estimated the final total dead would "max" at 2,500 tops.

Britain's Blair also misled the British public over the exaggerated death claims to justify Clinton's War.

The report claimed that Clinton's War, never based on national security, relied wholly on the "humanitarian" motive.

Collateral damage and infrastructure damage in Yugoslavia proceeded for 78 days. Thousands of innocent civilians were killed. Schools, hospitals, bridges, factories, homes, and water and power facilities were destroyed.

Environmental damage was horrendous. The Danube River was polluted and largely not navigable because of busted bridges. Most damage was caused by only "relatively accurate" bombs dropped from 15,000 feet and cruise missiles fired from many miles away.

Estimates of rebuilding costs were estimated at upwards of $100 billion, although guesstimates at human costs were forever inestimable.

In Kosovo, the situation was worse. Unexploded and American cluster bombs and mines posed a continuing hazard. Schlafly's report reported that "the humanitarian crisis did not exist—until after the U. S.—NATO air strikes began and Serbs began expelling Abanians from Kosovo."

As of December 1999, peacekeepers have been unable to restrain Albanian Muslims from heaping revenge by murdering Serbs and burning their homes and churches. The report claimed that more Serb civilians were killed in Kosovo than ethnic Albanians before the air strikes began.

Schlafly labeled the Clinton-Albright policy on Kosovo as totally absurd
A fantasy "forcing Albanians and Serbs to live in peace" will provoke and perturb
> Neither side wants any of the other,
> Multiethnic nonsense is pure pother,
And to impose "globocop and social worker will" is fatally destined to disturb

Schlafly's report also cited Berger who had given a speech at a Council of Foreign Relations meeting that Clinton's foreign policy was based on "engagement," which equated to "meddling in the internal affairs of sovereign nations." Berger forecast that America would be engaged in Yugoslavia for the rest of our lives.

An 11-year old Albanian girl in Kosovo was sexually assaulted and killed by Staff Sergeant Ronghi charged Colonel Golson of the U. S. military command wrote Eddy. Staff Sergeant Ronghi was a member of NATO's 50,000 member peacekeeping force stationed in Kosovo.

The girl's body was found in the country near Vitina. Her face was battered and bruised. It appeared she had been raped before being killed. Neighbors told her father that his daughter had been killed in the basement of an apartment building.

Serbian television criticized the case and "exposed it as an unprecedented disgrace." Serbs were extremely dissatisfied with the efforts of the peacekeepers to keep peace.

How this incident would affect future relations between Albanians and Americans was unknown at the time.

"Peaceful Coexistence" Continues in Kosovo since NATO's Occupation

After two Serbs were killed in a bus ambush, they retaliated and killed nine Albanians in the worst violence since the end of hostilities described

Gall. The divided city of Mitrovica was the scene of the fierce fighting with 9,000 Serbs and 90,000 Albanians separated at opposite sides of a bridge spanning the Ibar River.

French peacekeepers had to fire tear gas to disperse 500 rioters at the bridge. The Serbs wanted Albanians living among them "removed" from the Serbian section of Mitrovica for self-survival purposes.

Both Serbs and Albanians called the French peacekeeping forces "ineffective" and not doing enough to protect people.

In addition to the bus ambush and street fighting deaths, there were explosions in apartment buildings, torched UN cars, burned houses and a café explosion that wounded 14 Serbs.

Williams reported on a "global security debate" that lambasted NATO's "first offensive military incursion" into a sovereign state as a "moral, misguided, expensive and an unfinished job that that left the potential for many future Balkan Wars."

The generals and political defense and security strategists gathered together and hoped for a "self-congratulatory celebration" of amity and determination of NATO's future. Instead, the post NATO conference criticized it for political cowardice and functioning as an excessive bureaucracy. Disagreements over a new Continental Army, independent of NATO and the U. S., plus U. S. determination to build an anti ballistic missile defense system despite vehement Russian objections were also aired.

Russia's General Ivashov called the Continental Army and U. S. IBM shield "songs of praise for warfare."

Defense Department Perle rebutted Ivashov but "shunned diplomatic advice from Russia that was bombing Chechnya into oblivion."

Senator Biden was saddened that "not enough was learned from Bosnia that applied to Kosovo." He charged that the establishment of a civilian police force to patrol Kosovo and Bosnia-Herzevinia had been unfulfilled. Biden also called Clinton's policy of "intervening without loss of life a horrible standard."

General Wesley Clark criticized NATO's cumbersome decision-making process and the dangers of incrementalism that tipped off the enemy thereby reducing the effectiveness of its offense.

Gilbert, ex British deputy defense minister, was dismayed it took 78 days for NATO, with the world's most advanced technology, to bring an isolated and impoverished nation like Serbia to its knees.

Germany's General Kaumann said, "Ground troops had to be committed to stop human rights violations or the whole thing is a sham."

Apparently with tongue in cheek, Defense Secretary Cohen and counterparts in British and Germany termed Kosovo a success because ethnic cleansing "stopped," state sponsored violence "ceased," the Serbian military withdrew and the refugees were home. Cohen expressed deep concern regarding the new Continental Army.

Cohen warned the Europeans the new "Continental Army" would duplicate existing NATO forces and divert funds needed to support NATO. He also mentioned the "go ahead" with development and deployment of a ground-based National Missile Defense (NMD); Clinton's "mini" program designed as political sop to the "maxi" Star Wars program. He acknowledged that "limited effective ABM defenses were technologically feasible" probably in view of the Pentagon's ongoing anti ballistic missile testing.

Cohen purposely neglected to mention that Europe's desire for a new, independent "Continental Army" was proposed as a heartening sign of second thoughts and the re-emergence of European nationalism to "get out from under the tentacles and control of NATO and the U. S."

French troops were caught up in a fierce skirmish between Serbs and Albanians in Mitrovica reported an Associated Press news item. French troops killed one Albanian and over a dozen people were wounded including two French soldiers. Seventeen others were arrested in open street fighting. The French peacekeepers had become more aggressive after being accused of being "too soft on violence."

Both Serbians and Albanians regarded Mitrovica as the "last" battlefield of Clinton's War in Kosovo.

Bluestein wrote that Milosevic was "having his way" with peacekeepers in the industrial city of Mitrovica. The Serb leader has a financial interest in the Trepca complex of mines and the smelter at Zvecan that processes ores trucked in by foreign companies.

Mitrovica, Serbia's only stronghold in Kosovo is where Milosevic had flaunted French peacekeepers and UN administrators by sending in Serbian police and paramilitary forces to harass and expel Albanians living in the Serbian section of the city.

French troops refused to act when Serbs began removing heavy processing equipment from the Albanian side of town and refused to transport a wounded man to a French field hospital.

It appeared that German General Reinhardt and frustrated international officials were abandoning the UN's commitment to "create and protect a multiethnic society in Kosovo." They favored a view that "mixing the ethnics was impossible and the only recourse to stopping the killing was to keep them apart."

With Albanians, Serbs and French soldiers being killed or wounded, the situation required a "resolute and strong KFOR presence, mediation, UN administration of the city and closing the mines and smelter according to Bluestein.

An anonymous Associated Press news item related that France was dispatching 600-700 troops and the U. S. "might" send a Marine Unit to quell the rising violence between Albanians and Serbs in Mitrovica. France already had 4,500 peacekeepers in Kosovo.

Defense Secretary Cohen said that Mitrovica was merely a flash point of short duration. He believed that a show of force would be essential to maintaining peace.

The ethnic situation between Albanians and Serbians in Kosovo appeared to have no end in sight reported the Associated Press. The 22nd

Marine Expeditionary Unit was stationed aboard ships in the Mediterranean and was potentially available as standby reinforcements.

Although NATO may have to quell ethnic flare-ups in Mitrovica, most European nations had little inclination to increase the number of troops in Kosovo. France was prepared to add 600 to 700 troops in Kosovo, however.

General Clark desired the extra French troops and sought 1,200 other troops, which included the heretofore-mentioned U. S. 22nd Marine Expeditionary Unit, placed on standby alert.

About 5,300 American troops were then serving as peacekeepers in Kosovo. Albright preferred more European troops serve and noted the American military contingent in Kosovo was the largest. Senator Warner was concerned for increased risks to U. S. armed force personnel in Kosovo.

Erlanger wrote that the failure of NATO to bring meaningful security, justice and freedom of civilian movement in Mitrovica had it "shook up." Ethnic strife continued undiminished and international police couldn't control it even with support of the peacekeepers.

European nations have not supplied adequate personnel, police officers and funds charged Albright. They retorted that they didn't want their military units to take real risks and complained that the U. S. was too prone to blame Milosevic for every problem.

Nearly 175 Albanians had fled from Dobrosin into Gnjilane, which is not far from Pristina provincial capital of Kosovo reported the Associated press. Many sporadic clashes have occurred between Albanian guerrillas and Serbian police.

The "new" KLA is called the Presevo, Medvedja and Bujanovac Liberation Army named after three towns mostly populated with Albanians. The towns are located in Serbia proper, just east of Kosovo's border.

The Albanian rebels were trying to protect their people from attacks by Serbs. Fears abounded that the clashes might lead to resumption of NATO attacks. The killings in Kosovo have been regular occurrences since Serbian troops were forced to withdraw in June 1999.

Other flash points included Gracanica where a Serbian Orthodox Monastery is located. NATO peacekeepers were forced to seal off the city. Serbs retaliated by setting up roadblocks on the highway to Pristina.

The United Nations asserted that Albanians continue a relentless campaign of terror to drive Serbs out of Kosovo wrote Layne. The ultimate intent appeared designed to goad NATO into renewed hostilities.

Clinton's goal to transform Kosovo into a multiethnic democracy was purely "mythical"
To resettle Albanians in the northern Serb section was shortsighted and "problematical"
    Caused the remaining Serbs to exit in haste,
    Left a "de facto" separatist distaste,
And lets the KLA to "ethnically cleanse" Serbs, Gypsies et al. with a win "antithetical"

The Clinton administration never quite understood the real nature of Balkan conflicts
That is, "rival ethnic groups are only secure with territorial control and constricts"
    Hardly "pseudo multiethnicity,"
    It's firmed on "ethnic exclusivity,"
Which is the "only foundation for enduring peace with centuries old hated foe addicts"

Layne wrote that Clinton involved the U. S. through ignorance and KLA manipulation
Rebels couldn't defeat the Serb Army without U. S.—NATO help in the confrontation
    It provoked the Serbs into brutal reprisals,
    Which led to "air strike and peacekeeper" arrivals,

Then smugly reveled that "clever" Clinton placed the blame on Milosevic's administration

European officials said the "KLA was the most dangerous fomenter" in the Balkans. It desired ethnic exclusivity in an independent Kosovo and planed to utilize it as the staging area to attain a Greater Albania consisting of Kosovo, Albania and sections of Serbia and Macedonia.

NATO was remiss in not controlling the non-democratic KLA because it feared enraging the KLA leadership that might engage in hostilities with the NATO peacekeepers.

The question remained, however: "Would the U. S. continue to allow the KLA to use it as a "stoop or fool," prepare to deploy troops in an open-ended commitment in Kosovo or inform the European Union that "it's their problem to solve?"

Chapter 8

Clinton's Imperialism in the Near East—A "Palestinian State"

The issue of the Palestinian State is discussed briefly beginning with a bit of Background, Broder's Report on The Palestinian State, Associated Press Perceptions and Author's Perception of a Separate Palestine.

Background

This chapter discusses Clinton's imperialism in the Near East. The volatile issue of a separate Palestinian State continues to fester in cyclical emergence, submergence, re-emergence and so forth. In actuality, the question of a Palestinian State began with the installation of Israel as a separate State without any humanitarian concern or provision for millions of Palestinians who occupied the same land in question for centuries. It's easy to look back to 1948 in hindsight and recall the "astute, forward-looking, globally oriented Western leaders and diplomats" who then established Israel as a separate nation and left the Palestinians to wallow in their forsaken misery. Had a Palestinian State then been established, over one-half century of Israeli –Palestinian hatred, rancor, distrust, terrorism, deaths, injuries, war and hundreds of billions in U. S. foreign aid bribery dispensed to maintain "peace" in the Middle East would have been obviated without doubt.

Broder's Report on the Palestinian State

Broder's column reported that outright Israel supporter, duplicitous Clinton planted the seeds of autonomy and independence and opined that "Palestinians should be able to settle wherever they want to live." Ostensibly, the global nation meddler preferred to have the "Palestinians spread throughout the Middle East." (Most likely, Clinton was in an ambiguous state, torn between his allegiance toward Israel, campaign donations and votes plus peaceful pursuit of the one-world objective.)

Officials in the White House and State Department, "essentially echoes of Clinton's policy," were understandably upset and issued immediate denials that any change in U. S. policy toward Israel was unaffected. The anonymous "They" thought that Israel and the Palestinians should resolve the matter. "They" even commented in true "spin-doctor or bail-out mode" that "Clinton had spoken imprecisely."

In his usual duplicitous manner, Clinton used such phrases as "a practical matter, nature of the settlement, how much land, how long they've been away, if they wish to go home and how it corresponded to where people lived before" to smoke screen and confuse the issue.

It appeared that clever, conniving Clinton was attempting to capitalize on the successful de facto tactic of "re-applying" Albanian immigrant suffusion in Kosovo" to the Israeli-Palestinian enigma. It seemed feasible, from Clinton's utterances that nation status for Israel—except in name only, would be "abandoned and submerged" to coveted border-less one-world hegemony.

Associated Press Perceptions

An anonymous Associated Press news item reported that Israel's Supreme Court ruled that Eiya Kaadan's parents can buy land in Katzia.

In 1994, the Israeli Lands Authority along with the Jewish Agency rejected the Kaadan's application to buy land. The ruling overturned a 52-year old state policy of restricting land sales to Arabs. The Israeli Arabs hailed the decision as a breakthrough in the struggle for equality. Arabs then constituted 20 percent of Israel's population of six million.

The decision ruled that restricting sales to Jews was not compatible with democracy or with the nation's character not to discriminate among its citizenry. It allowed Arabs to buy land in Jewish communities unless a legitimate reason for segregation existed. Kibbutzim, communal farms, would remain segregated, however.

Critics of the ruling feared Arab majorities established in key areas like the West Bank and Gaza Strip would "undermine" Israeli's security. Others dreaded, over time, that land adjacent to the Palestinian entity would become less Jewish. 'One legislator, Yehezkel, promised to submit legislation to "sidestep" the ruling.

(It seemed apparent that the ruling could be the beginning of the end of "nationalist" Israel. Arab pleas for "autonomy and independence" might develop later on akin to the Albanian's "struggle in Kosovo." Perhaps that is what Israelis feared most.)

Author's Perception of the Palestinian State

The real issue was, of course, was to denationalize, desovereignize and multiethnically inundate or suffuse a "UN-created" sovereign nation presumably secure under the slogan, "umbrella of international peace." In this manner, the issues of a separate Palestinian nation might be neutralized as a non-issue and the erstwhile "thorn in the Mid East since its inception, Israel" seen my many observers, might also be pruned from its "favored nation" political status.

Plainly, Clinton's "uber alles" policy of border-less nations would temporarily "dismiss or eliminate the ostensible need for a Palestinian State by multiethnicizing Israel with Palestinians." At the same time, it would weaken Israel's influence and importance in the process and set the stage for future "justification" to interfere militarily should refugee inundation attain a "de facto disproportion of Palestinians" who demanded autonomy and independence. The intentionally created "crisis" would then have to be resolved by "U. S.—NATO intervention." The scenario would not be unlike the Albanian suffusion of immigrants into Kosovo with subsequent rebellion for autonomy and ultimate independence.

Clinton's pronouncements were essentially responsive modifications of cohort activist Hillary's earlier "call for an independent Palestinian nation," which evoked immediate, transient, tremulous trepidation in the White House, State Department, United Nations, Israel and its Zionist supporters. As a consequence, disputation regarding two nationalistic-oriented nations, "one real and one potential," would become moot. Hillary, too, in a trial balloon foreign policy move would have been extricated from the political digs and abyss she recently and brilliantly excavated for herself.

It should be borne in mind at all times that "no nation is immune from submergence and enslavement to one-world government control with residual, euphemistic nationalism remaining in name only"—if global government proponents have their way! Global government aficionados have already demonstrated their intentions—implemented by military force when necessary as in Kosovo.

Chapter 9

East Timor's Quest for Autonomy and Independence

The quest for East Timor's "Independence" is discussed under the headings of Introduction, Clough on East Timor's "Challenge of Separatism," International Military and Education Training—IMET, International Pressure Caused Indonesian President to "Invite" UN Peacekeepers, IFOR's Composition and the Invasion of East Timor, Criticisms of Clinton's Action Toward East Timor and IFOR's Peaceful Invasion and Aftermath.

Introduction

Fresh and flushed from his imperialistic "air strikes" victory over Serbia and in the name of de facto Albanian immigration suffusion of Kosovo, Clinton issued pronouncements and was primed to extend his One World tentacles toward the Far East, specifically East Timor—a province of Indonesia. Rebel "separatists" in East Timor were "seeking autonomy and independence" from the sovereign nation of Indonesia. The situation was analogous to the recent Albanian rebel uprising in Kosovo, province of Serbia. The tense, "civil war" situation had become another "crisis and a perilous threat to international peace" despite the fact that most people never heard of East Timor.

The plight of East Timor was a relatively "safe" internationalist intervention; it obviously posed a minimal amount of domestic protest in the U. S. Its citizens, for the most part, never heard of East Timor due to de-emphasis of Geography and History being taught in most "dumbed down or revisionist" courses in American educational institutions and perhaps was linked to Clinton's long-time nexus with the Riaddys of Indonesia. For the first time, the United Nations' "IFOR, International Force for Peace was "authorized by a dubious request" to meddle into the internal affairs and civil strife of a Far East sovereign nation—Indonesia.

The "uber alles" United Nations led by Clinton was once again in relentless pursuit of one-world hegemony under the guise of the banner, "peace throughout the world with national sovereignty belittled, besmirched and bedamned."

Clough on East Timor's "Challenge of Separatism"

Clough suggested that Indonesia could be another "challenge of separatism." East Timor was the focal point and a vote to decide independence would be taken on August 30th. The UN would supervise the referendum and "favored" independence, of course. Indonesia said it would accept the vote for independence should it occur

The U. S and its allies were already developing contingency plans for conducting a possible "peaceful invasion" in East Timor in anticipation of the politically contrived "crisis."

Aceh and Irian Java were two other provinces in rebellion and seeking independence from Indonesia that the government would refuse to accept.

Separation and "de facto" weakening of nationalism was abetted by the growing strength of pro-democracy groups, human rights violations, various crimes tribunals, unstable finances, flight of capital, currency depreciation, lost economic opportunity, decline of unconditioned foreign aid and political instability that could cost dearly.

Indonesia may have to grant greater autonomy, cultural and self-determination to separatists in order to demonstrate that the East Timorese were better off remaining part of Indonesia.

The U. S. and the UN could offer the usual bribes of diplomacy, which included economic and financial aid to Indonesia if they allowed autonomy and self-rule but not independence. "Separatists" (unlike those in Kosovo), however, would not receive foreign aid if they broke away.

International Military and Education Training— IMET

A column by Marshall and Richter revealed that the Pentagon's investment in training foreign officers including Indonesians had failed. The millions spent were supposed to train them for the military and plant seeds of American values and influence. Unfortunately, attempts by the Indonesian government to end the violence in East Timor failed and outbreaks of civil violence continued.

An unnamed congressional staff member who monitored the International Military Education and Training program, IMET, for 10 years remarked on its "complete lack of utility, at least in Indonesia." U. S. officials added that after 15 months, IMET provided little return during political convulsion in Indonesia that forced President Suharto from power. IMET spent $50 million during fiscal year 1998-99 and educated 9,000 military personnel from 100 countries.

Clinton accused the Indonesian Army of abetting the violence in East Timor. In retaliation, "uber alles" Clinton then announced an immediate freeze on arms sales that continued in 1999 and suspended inter-military operations with Indonesia.

International Pressure Caused Indonesian President to "Invite" UN Peace Keepers

Indonesia succumbed to intense pressure from global leaders and allowed an international peacekeeping force into the country to restore order in East Timor wrote Lekic. Naturally nettlesome nation meddler Clinton, then in Australia sounded off and said, "Some presence of U. S. ground forces may be required." They would serve only in a support role to "fly other nations' ground forces" to East Timor.

President Habibie commented that the "trumped up request" was made because Indonesian troops had been unsuccessful in quelling the civil war and he wanted to end the crisis. He also said that Indonesian troops had been stymied by "psychological difficulties in dealing with a very complex problem."

The UN's quickly justified its urgency for meddling in another civil war by immediately enumerating the usual number of "justifiable culprits"—human rights violations, deaths, injuries, property destruction, shortage of food-shelter-medicine and mounting numbers of refugees.

Akin to Bosnia and Kosovo, the priority for peacekeepers was intended to "disarm anti-independence militias and dedicated guerrillas." The UN had to save them from themselves! Anti-independence leaders accused the UN of "rigging" the independence vote and threatened to shoot UN troops.

Like Clinton, a number of global leaders applauded the decision that led to invasion of another sovereign country's province via an "imposed peace by military invasion." The "spontaneously" planned invasion was another rung in the one-world ladder attempts to destroy, minimize and/or neutralize nationalism.

Simultaneously, or was it just coincidence that Australian troops were on standby alert with its warships just a day's sail away? Apparently, UN involvement had been actively preparing for and abetting the situation before being "officially asked to participate." Ground forces from

Malaysia, New Zealand, France, Thailand, Canada and the Philippines were expected to invade East Timor momentarily.

IFOR's Composition and the Invasion of East Timor

Indonesian foreign minister Alatas, asked UN's Annan for assistance and was informed that an international force would be welcomed penned Crossette. A British—U. S. draft designated an Aussie Major General to command the international force. Although not setting conditions. Alatas preferred troops from the Association of Southeast Asian Nations like Malaysia, Thailand, Singapore, Philippines and British Ghurka troops in Brunei. It was hypocritically presented as an "Asian" not a "global" crisis you see. Some Indonesians considered Australia as a "provocative choice" for military command because it supported East Timor's independence.

France would send token military advisors and the U. S. would furnish planes to transport troops and equipment. Indonesian nationalists did not want troops as part of IFOR from America, New Zealand, Portugal and other non-Asian nations for reasons of prejudice against Indonesia. (Perhaps they remembered the close ties that existed between Clinton and the Riaddys.) Portuguese troops were also shunned because East Timor was a former Portugal colonial power.

Fifteen hours after its introduction, the UN approved an international force to "enforce" peace in East Timor and bring those responsible to justice. Australia would lead a multinational force of 3,000 troops and provide up to 4,500 soldiers.

An Associated press release said that soldiers from "France to Thailand" would be sent to rescue thousands of starving East Timorese whom fled to the hills from its capital, Dili. East Timorese rebel leader Gusman said, "He wouldn't return until it was safe."

Pro-Indonesian militia had shot and butchered thousands of people ever since the East Timorese voted for independence. Meanwhile, the UN was busy readying aircraft to supply food to the refugees.

Lamb's column described how Indonesian troops were leaving East Timor with tons of material after igniting their compound. The troops threatened refugees and burned homes as they withdrew.

Australian Major General Cosgrove, UN commander, led 2,000 peace-keepers as the first wave of a force destined to grow to 7,500 representing 20 nations. Meanwhile martial law in East Timor had been revoked and the responsibility for security was transferred to the IFOR. Peacekeepers and Indonesian soldiers were patrolling the streets of Dili.

Criticism of Clinton's Actions toward East Timor

Greenhut decried the Clinton administration for defying the founders' warnings of foreign entanglements. He charged that it continued to meddle in foreign civil wars without conducting serious debate in the Congress or with the public. It meddled in the internal affairs of nations under the guises of "protecting international order, stopping ethnic cleansing and upholding democratic values."

Greenhut thought the U. S. was and is "not the world's sovereign" or possessed the right to intervene in foreign nations for any presumptive "noble" purpose due to its military supremacy.

Columnist Greenhut wondered where Clinton's "self-ordained" admin-istration

    Obtained the "inherent right" to determine what is best for each nation

        Pursued its policy of dastardly destruction

        Inflicted "collateral damage" sans compunction,

    Defied the Constitution and deployed troops without war's declaration

In Kosovo, NATO forces "failed" to destroy the Serbian military
Were forced to focus on civilian targets somewhat arbitrary
    Bombed utilities, public transportation,
    Plants and factories into obliteration,
In order to justify a "success and moral victory" quite contrary

There is nothing "defensive" in sending U. S. troops "far and wide"
Because—into endless global meddling we continue to slide
    Human rights, the "new justification"
    For "Clinton's Wars" requires subjugation,
Aimed at global hegemony that no "free nation" should abide

IFOR's Peaceful Invasion and Aftermath

Mydans reported that the IFOR led by Australian Lieutenant-Colonel Welch took charge in Dili as Indonesian soldiers departed and East Timorese refugees emerged from hiding places.

The East Timorese immediately ignited into a spontaneous celebration that grew and grew. With celebrants waving the red, green and white flag of independence, the celebration ended abruptly with the advent of night because "they were still afraid of the dark."

The Associated Press related that East Timorese in Dili looted a warehouse, stole orange colored tarpaulins and coffee as IFOR "looked on." The refugees were returning from the hills seeking materials to build shelters as protection against the elements. Children helped tote the tarpaulins used to wrap 110-pound bags of prized coffee—one of East Timor's cash exports.

UN's Wimhurst said the problems in East Timor were "very big" and the "humanitarian crisis more serious than anticipated." Most villages had been severely damaged and/or burned. Some East Timorese who had been "deported" were replaced with people sympathetic to Indonesia.

Spencer wrote that IFOR's Major General Cosgrove and Indonesia's Major General Syahnakri met behind closed doors in Dili to discuss a "change of command." Details were not disclosed. Only 1,500 Indonesian troops out of 20,000 still remained and would stay until November 1999 when the Indonesian government ratified East Timor's independence. Solving the problems of rebuilding, starvation, food airdrops, returning refugees and war crimes charges had just begun.

The UN prepared to "look into" atrocities committed by Indonesian soldiers and militia in East Timor reported the Associated Press. People were furious that the bodies of two nuns, five church workers and students, a journalist and a driver were found floating in a river. They had been delivering food and "meds" to refugees. Hundreds of mourners were in the procession to the cemetery for proper burial.

The IFOR landed Blackhawk helicopters and swept through the village of Com. The ominous looking helicopters hovered over the area and provided immediate support and security for people obviously stressed out. Officers parleyed with the guerrilla organization, Falintil, but did not attempt to disarm its members. Many Indonesians were disturbed by IFOR's "selective inaction" because it disdained "neutrality." (It was reminiscent of KFOR's benign attitude toward the KLA's revengeful actions in Kosovo.)

Secretary General Annan presented a plan for the UN to take complete control of East Timor and steer it toward independent nation status over two to three years related the Associated Press. UN control of civil administration and defense were deemed "absolutely necessary" because of the extreme chaos that existed.

The UN plan would be debated in the UN and Washington, D. C. It was expected the plan would cost $1 billion. At the same time, Congress preferred to pay 25 percent, not 31 percent, for UN's peacekeeping operations of sovereign nation meddling.

Major General Cosgrove planned to disarm both pro-Indonesian and pro-independence fighters as a security measure in rebuilding East Timor according to the Associated Press. He wanted the violence halted.

Cosgrove was well aware that militiamen were still terrorizing about 200 refugee camps and impeding their return to East Timor.

The U. S. deployed helicopters and support personnel as part of IFOR. Three hundred (300) troops including 120 communication specialists and 24 "experts in civil-military matters" to help with logistics and intelligence were in the mix. Four Stallion helicopters were also aboard the U. S. S. Belleau Wood waiting deployment.

UN's Barton said that more than 200,000 East Timorese fled to West Timor, which is controlled by Indonesia.

Indonesia accepted "self-rule" for East Timor wrote an anonymous source. Guerrilla chief, Gusman, freed from two years detention, emerged as leader of the "new" East Timor nation. The guerrillas had been fighting for independence from Indonesia since Portugal departed in 1975.

Perhaps 200,000 East Timorese were killed or died from disease or starvation since Indonesia annexed East Timor as its 27th province. Thousands of Indonesian soldiers perished as well.

A separate East Timor began when a referendum vote of 78.5 percent held on August 30, 1999 favored independence. The vote infuriated Indonesian soldiers who proceeded to destroy 70 percent of East Timor's buildings and forced most of its 800,000 thousand residents into refugee status. Soon after the last Indonesian soldier departed, a spontaneous celebration began

Subsequently, 7,500 IFOR troops deployed in East Timor humiliated Indonesia and aroused inherent nationalism. Then a parliamentary election held on October 20th installed a Muslim cleric, Wahid, as president of Indonesia, the world's fourth largest nation.

Guerrilla Chief Gusman and President Wahid hoped to establish "friendly and cooperative" relations and become neighbors.

Chapter 10

Aceh, Chechnya and other "Provinces Possibly Ripe" for Nation Meddling

The provinces of both Aceh, Indonesia and Chechnya, Russia were "ripe" for the international nation meddlers. Obviously, the case of Aceh was more tolerable and safer than the situation in Chechnya because U. S.—NATO are nowhere near inclined to confront directly powerful Red Russia.

Aceh

Another province in Indonesia, Aceh, emboldened and spurred by East Timor's successful breakaway and quest for independence, was now striving for the same status wrote Lamb. Culmination of Aceh's struggle for independence could lead ultimately to war, autonomy or independence.

Anti-government rebel forces were increasingly confident they would succeed. They resented the fact that small numbers of Acehnese were killed daily in this resource-rich province. In December 1999, one million people rallied in a call for independence.

Professor Winters, Northwestern University, said that Indonesia needed Aceh more than the Aceh needed Indonesia. It has the potential to create a Gross Domestic Product larger than the rest of Indonesia. It generates

$4 million per day from the Arun natural gas fields in northern Aceh. A loss of Aceh would likely restore power to the military and loss of a fledgling "democracy."

Indonesian president, Wahid, announced a separate Aceh wouldn't be tolerated and offered a referendum for autonomy only. The Indonesian Army had brutally treated the Acehnese for a long time. . In order to appease the Acehnese, Wahid appointed an Acehnese as deputy military commander, started a $60 million railway project, allowed the island of Sabang to become a free trade zone and arranged a deal where the Acehenese could keep 75 percent of its forestry, agriculture, oil and gas earnings. It established a civilian military tribunal to prosecute soldiers found guilty of civil rights violations.

Wahid had also traveled extensively from Washington to Manila seeking pledges of support for a unified Indonesia. In a global sense thus far, the pledges have effectively isolated the Free Aceh Movement.

The Acehnese were undecided whether Aceh should be an Islamic state, a rigid monarchy or a democracy. Rebel leader Syafie wanted sovereignty for Aceh. He craved cooperation from other nations especially the U. S. and invited them to come and inspect the brutal conditions first hand.

International silence and inaction on Aceh has been partly due to its location on the Straits of Malacca, one of the four choke points on the international waterways, and extremely essential to Indonesian integrity. Aceh's independence could encourage other movements for independence in Irian Jaya, Riau and elsewhere. Regional unrest would Balkanize Indonesia and destabilizes Southeast Asia politically and economically.

Further, rebel forces numbered only approximately 1,000 members— its most glaring weakness. They had engaged in brutalities as burning uncooperative villagers, converting villagers into refugees and moving them to refugee camps and "demanding " donations of money and materials in a door-to-door campaign in Banda Aceh in order to "control" the population. The rebels often "provoked" attacks on soldiers who now spent more time in barracks as per Wahid's orders.

Indonesia gained its independence from Dutch colonialism in December 1949. Indonesia's first president, Sukarno, promised Aceh autonomy, a promise never kept. Suharto, Indonesia's second president, vowed to raise the living standards and increase religious freedom. Instead, he took control of Aceh's vital resources and sent the army in to crush the rebels who demanded imposition of Islamic laws.

Aceh first rebelled against the Indonesian government in 1953. It has been designated as a military zone ever since 1989.

The situation in Aceh sounded much like the "crisis" in Kosovo. The rebels, akin to the KLA and Muslim religious practice, suffuse the province, want autonomy and/or independence and are willing to fight for those objectives.

Chechnya

Prime Minister Putin said that Russia would "not" pay heed to the UN or Annan's pressure tactics to stop the war in Chechnya wrote Dixon. Just as NATO paid no heed to Russia's opposition to air strikes in Kosovo, Russia wouldn't negotiate with Chechen terrorists.

The Russian people backed the government in its stand on the six-week war. Putin insisted "the war was purely an internal matter and he wouldn't negotiate with bandits."

Annan argued that innocent people were being killed and excessive force was being used to destroy terrorists. Putin responded by saying "Western moral persuasion lacked much moral force in Russia."

Analyst Kremenyich called Western pressure "totally counterproductive, shortsighted and stupid." Western pressure would only goad Russia to decimate Chechnya if need be and its position was irreversible.

A hale and combative Yeltsin informed European leaders at a summit meeting of the Organization for Security and Cooperation in Europe (OSCE) in Istanbul they had "no right to fault Russia for its war (in Chechnya) on bandits and murderers." He labeled calls for peace "hopelessly naïve" and "the plight of civilians" didn't justify Western meddling. It seemed that Yeltsin acted like a patriotic nationalist, not cowed by "one-world meddlers."

Clinton tried to use "moral considerations" to justify meddling in the internal affairs of sovereign nations that included air strikes in Kosovo and public criticism in the case of Chechnya. Yeltsin, however, ridiculed the notion of "humanitarian interference" and had no inclination to negotiate with bandits and terrorists. Yeltsin would only bend slightly by agreeing to allow a representative from the OSCE to visit Chechnya.

An ailing Yeltsin warned and admonished Clinton for his criticism for Russia's stance on Chechnya wrote Dorgan. "Clinton will not dictate Russia's policy. It is for us to dictate," said Yeltsin. He reminded Clinton that Russia is a "great power and possesses a nuclear arsenal." Prime Minister Putin sought to calm the chill in relationships between U. S. and Russia.

China's foreign minister Quiyue supported Russia's nationalist efforts to maintain national unification and territorial integrity. China, too, is disdainful of Western interference in other nations' domestic matters.

Yeltsin was in China at the time busy "cementing" relationships and meeting with President Zemin, then separately with Premier Rongii and Li.

Deputy Secretary of State Talbot accused Russia of "indiscriminate killing in Chechnya," then left without making progress over a major arms control treaty penned Bohlen. Clinton wanted to modify the 1972 ABM treaty over Russia's objections in order to build a "watered down" defense against long-range missile attacks from terrorists. He also said the Reds violated international norms by treating Chechen civilians as terrorists.

Putin was more interested in reducing the nuclear warhead arsenals of both countries to 3500 weapons by year 2002.

Meanwhile, General Kuzantsev said Grozy would be conquered within a week by special operations, not by storm.

While in Moscow, Albright's intent was to "size up Putin and push arms control" reported Schweid. She was critical of the war in Chechnya and said Russia faced "international isolation." Many U. S. appeals to end the conflict had failed but economic sanctions were ruled out in any case.

She wanted to discuss sharp cuts in ICBMs of both countries and urge Putin to "agree" to a modest $6.6 billion anti-ballistic missile plan for the United States. (Since when is any nation including the U. S. obliged to ask another nation, even Russia, to "agree" to properly defend itself? That notion is totally ludicrous.)

One world zealot Madeline was concerned that "democratically elected governments were turning to authoritarianism to solve economic anxieties." (What drivel? They were only voicing nationalist, not one-world concerns and not eager to slave like submit to non-elected international appointees.) Clever, conniver, cowardly Clinton had not directly confronted Russia on Chechnya but had delayed several loans requested by Russia from the IMF and the Export—Import Bank. He mentioned Russia's economic mismanagement and corruption as "reasons for the delay."

Albright believed there was "no military solution" to the Chechen problem reported the Associated Press on February 1, 2000. "Let's bomb the hell out of them" Albright charged the conflict resulted in an incredible amount of misery on civilians by indiscriminate targeting. It was a hypocritical comment uttered by Albright on "collateral damage" after the havoc and devastation U. S.—NATO air strikes inflicted on thousands of Serb civilians including women, children, elderly et al. in Kosovo and also in Afghanistan and Sudan.

Foreign Minister Ivanov replied that Russia had to move firmly against rebellious terrorism, a move shared by other governments and Russian nationalists. Apparently, Russian wasn't worried about a military confrontation with the U. S. or NATO since their chances of involvement were essentially "slim and none." The West is compelled to view Russia as a "friendly enemy" most essential to an all-encompassing "mini one-world U. S—Europe." Other arguments are specious, political hot air mouthings.

Albright retorted that Russia's actions wouldn't eliminate terrorism but would cause "diplomatic isolation"—akin to the same tactic used to threaten Austria.

She also sidestepped the Star Wars anti ballistic missile defense issue but "linked" it with further reductions of nuclear arsenals. Clinton and Putin might meet in Moscow after Russia's national elections were over to "discuss the linkage."

An Associated Press news blurb scribed the seizure of the last rebel stronghold in Grozny, capital of Chechnya. President Putin declared an end to the laborious military drive to capture the Chechen capital although independent sources had not yet confirmed the claim.

Grozny, capital of Checknya, had been reduced to a barely inhabitable wasteland after years of war wrote Bagrov and Merkushev. From 1994-1996, Chechnya had attained "de facto" independence and was basically ungovernable. Russia's latest offensive reduced Grozny's population from 400,000 to 40,000 citizens who now live in bombed out apartment building basements and other devastated buildings.

Three days after Russian troops reclaimed total control of Grozny, its central city
    It was an endless panorama of disaster and ruin that exuded great pity
        Rotting human flesh emitted a sickly smell,
        Graffiti gruesomely proclaimed "Welcome to Hell,"
Buildings damaged beyond repair and gaping shell holes everywhere from war's rapacity
    Damage inflicted on Grozny was roughly estimated near $1 billion. No estimates of the numbers killed and wounded were released to the public. In addition, no relief agencies had yet reached the capital.

In Grozny, 40 thousand civilians had been trapped during the siege assault
    Then many elderly and children were relieved Russia's attack did halt

They staggered toward military soup kitchens for some food,
Ate buckwheat porridge and bread, drank tea that tasted so good,
Couldn't fathom why they deserved devastation and ruin, were wrong
and at fault

The Russian military insisted that "shelling was the only way" to
destroy the rebel's elaborate fortifications. They denied using grenades
against civilians or using women as human shields. The troops were busy
"mopping up" remnants of rebel resistance

Chief Russian administrator, Koshman, wanted to raze Grosny and
move the capitol to Gudermes in eastern Chechnya, but military chief
Gantamirov wanted the city to be rebuilt.

An anonymous Associated Press news item reported Russian air and
ground forces were seizing the high ground and battering rebel strong-
holds in the mountains south of Grozny. About 8,000 rebels, skilled in
guerrilla warfare, were believed holed up in the rugged mountains.

Prospects for many refugees returning to devastated Grosny were considered doubtful. Some Russian officials even doubted the city would be
rebuilt due to lack of money.

Chechen rebels shot down a Russian helicopter and killed 15 soldiers
related an Associated Press blurb. The helicopter was spotting targets
for Russian military aircraft and artillery. About 7,000 rebels retreated
to the mountains and hoped to wage an extended guerrilla war against
the Russians.

Meanwhile, Russian forces were in the process of sealing off Grozny
until March 1, 2000. They mopped up pockets of resistance and defused
land mines.

Back in Moscow, 100 protesters demanded an end to the war and to
Russia's mandatory military draft.

A graphic video portrayed mutilated Chechen men tossed into a mass
grave reported McMahon. A German correspondent said soldiers told
him the bodies were Chechen soldiers killed in battle and brought in from

south Chechnya. The mutilations were explained because a number of soldiers had been dragged on the ground by rope or wire. The video stirred international pressure on Russia that promptly dismissed it as propaganda and/or a hoax.

Human Rights Watch charged that Russian troops executed Chechen civilians during and after the capture of Grozny. Other charges leveled against the troops involved stealing money and looting homes.

Moscow also rejected these charges as Western propaganda and asserted that "outside, independent monitors" were unnecessary.

Albright demanded an investigation into the charges. UN's Solana was concerned about human rights abuses and urged Russian cooperation—an unlikely prospect.

An anonymous From Times news item stated that President Putin was considering possible changes in policy on Chechnya. Britain's Blain visited Putin and was concerned over humanitarian violations. He wanted Russia to "engage with the rest of the world."

Putin told Blain that Russia was prepared to cooperate with the Red Cross, Organization for Security and Cooperation in Europe, United Nations and the Council of Europe. The latter had already visited Chechnya and was "shocked at the devastation."

The five-month war began in September 1999 and fierce fighting still continues between Russian troops and Chechen rebels in Chechnya and nearby mountains in the Vedeno region.

Chapter 11

Austria, Latest Upstart Nation Poised to Defy "U. S.—NATO Meddling"

Austria is the latest European nation, along with Russia, ready to defy "U. S.—NATO meddling" in the internal affairs of a sovereign nation. The usual threats of "diplomatic isolation, cuts in economic-military aid, bribes, loans, forgiveness of loans, outright largesse, racist and xenophobic accusations" were the preferred "diplomatic weapons" used to discourage renegade nations from preserving their nationalist sovereign integrity in anything but "euphemistic" terms. Renegade nations are obliged to "heel" to the dictates of "U. S.—European mini one-world proponents," else they might be "militarily invaded" in order to preserve and satisfy the objectives of globally bent, arrogant, non-elected, militant "peaceful" ideologues.

Inundation of immigrants, legal and illegal, across "borderless" countries and UN approved "democratic" governments appeared to be among the main strategies and diplomatic devices for "denationalizing" sovereign countries, weakening them in the process, leaving them "nations in name only" and subjugating them to the dictates of a tyrannical global government. It is the main reason for the policy of encouraging free and widespread "de facto and de jure" immigrant movements everywhere—sovereignty and national laws be damned and implementation of so-called democracy merely a myth. Globalists disdainfully equate "nationalism" to "racist and xenophobic behavior."

With steely resolve evident in applying its "borderless nation "policy, the European Union (EU) countries warned Austria of "diplomatic isolation," if Haider's anti immigration Freedom Party as part of a democratically elected coalition government proceeded with its policies. The EU wouldn't accept "any" bilateral official contracts at a political level but would only receive them at a technical level wrote McNeil, Jr.

Haider retorted that if he and President Klestil bowed to foreign pressure, "then we might as well abolish democracy in this country straight away."

Portugals' Prime Minister Guterres made it known that "behavior of a racist or xenophobic character would not be tolerated in the European Union."

Austria's foreign minister, Schuessel was shocked at the announcement by Guterres, which was made without first consulting Austria, a member state of the European Union.

Haider's Freedom Party favored cutting off "eastern European" immigration to Austria. Haider desired to prevent inundation of immigrants from Eastern Europe and opposed European Union expansion.

An anonymous news item penned that Haider's Freedom Party and Schuessel's Peoples Party would form a government coalition and present it to President Klestil for approval. Klestil's approval was likely.

According to the mood in Austria, if a new election were called, the Freedom Party would likely prevail and Haider would become chancellor.

Unnamed U. S. officials said that a government with the Freedom Party would likely "affect our bilateral relationship"

Foreign Minister Schuessel called "any foreign attempts at meddling to 'stop' the coalition totally inappropriate."

Austria's president, Klestil, was scheduled to meet with Haider and Schuessel, sign a "declaration of values of 'undefined' European democracy" soon to be approved by the new government reported the Associated Press.

Meanwhile, 10,000 people assembled before the People's Party head-quarters to protest the new coalition arrangement.

Klestil's declaration was intended to "spare Austria from diplomatic and political isolation." Haider and Schuessl uttered assurances that democratic values would be respected, which didn't assure protesters.

Israel called Haider "dangerous" and recalled its ambassador. Portuguese and Norwegian officials were wary and anticipated the coalition would result in diplomatic isolation for Austria.

Rabinbach wrote that the European Union and the U. S. would virtu-ally "isolate" Austria, a member of the EU, because of its new coalition government. Italy's Prime Minister D'Alema called the "political isolation" action a stand for "standards and values of European unity and a refusal to brook faint remembrances of Europe's totalitarian and racist past."

Many people opposed the European Union's direct interference with the outcome of a democratic election in peaceful and stable Austria. They feared a disturbing precedence was being established.

European Union members were quick to dredge up Austria's Nazi past and Haider's xenophobic, "borderless nation" slogans that might ignite similar movements elsewhere. They dreaded any sympathetic statements on behalf of the Waffen SS and Wehrmach veterans as well as Haider's political excesses.

Rabinbach cited fears of the radical right's resurgent nationalism with France's Jean-Marie Le Pen movement, Slovakia's Meclar, Italy's neofascist Fini (National Alliance Party) and Russia's Zhirinorsky. The growth of Germany's extreme right due to scandal surrounding former Chancellor Kohl was also dreaded by present chancellor, Schroeder. Rabinbach recalled that predominantly Social Democrats and liberals had ruled Europe since 1945.

Rabinbach perceived Haider as quite popular with the corporate elite, those under 30, rather mediagenic, not strongly ideological, economically liberal and frustrated with political patronage of jobs dispensed by the entrenched two-party system. Haider promised to play by democratic rules.

On the other hand, Haider's far right Freedom Party is the largest in Europe and second largest in Austria. He denounced the European Union as "corrupt." Schuessel also stated, "Austria does not have to liked."

The European Union's "real" concerns are, of course, Haider's threat to the policy of borderless nations, suffusion of immigrants wherever and whenever, resurgence of nationalism with its possible spread to other nations and resistance to the notion of a unified, mini U. S.—European one-world begemony. Any outspoken, vociferous and active patriotic form of nationalism would simply not be tolerated. Member nations must "knuckle under" as helots to tyrannical United Nations hegemony.

Patently, EU's policy of "borderless nations" equates any anti immigrant stance to racism and xenophobia, which is inimical to denationalization. The EU envisions no place for xenophobic, racist or extreme nationalists in the "authoritarian—or euphemistically called European 'democratic' one-world government." The authoritarian "far right," not the communists posed the greatest threat in the past? The only extremists are "far right" proponents, not the ruthless "peaceful" one-worlders who fervently desire to "enslave all nations and destroy national sovereignty everywhere"— with military might when necessary.

Over 150,000 Viennese demonstrators protested peaceful inclusion of the far right Freedom Party in the Austrian Government despite being legitimately elected reported Sliva. They "feared 'right wing nationalism' might creep into Austria again." The demonstrators vowed that fascists would never again threaten democracy in Austria. Protests were held throughout Vienna at such famous landmarks as "Heroes' Square" and the parliament building.

One colorful banner proclaimed, "Being ruled by the Freedom Party haunts our soul." Other banners had statements that "feared rule by black and blue hands, and "help retain our human dignity."

The protests stemmed from Haider's opposition to immigration, rapid European Union expansion and previous praise of certain Nazi policies.

Chancellor Schuessel expected the protests to wane after the "generations from the far-left, hippies, the youth and the Internet have had their fling."

Williams wrote the demonstrators vowed never to allow the "fascists" to threaten democracy in Austria again. The coalition of the Freedom Party and Peoples Party now rule over Austria after 30 years of "centrist" rule.

In retaliation to the "legitimate election of the Freedom Party," the arrogant, petulant, ruler-supreme European Union imposed "diplomatic isolation," acknowledged tourism had been hurt and asked member nations to freeze official contracts with the Viennese government.

Outrage was directed toward Schuessel because the Freedom Party heads now control half of the government ministries. Some protester placard banners read, "Haider is Hitler" and "No to racism."

Haider charged that SOS Mitmensch, an immigration advocacy group, paid many protesters $130.00 per day. Some Austrians liked the idea of protesting but didn't think it would make a difference. Many other citizens thought like Haider but "didn't dare speak up." Still others wanted the protesters to calm down and give the coalition government a chance to prove it's not neo-fascist.

President Klestil secured assurances from Albright and European leaders to maintain reasonable relations with Austria, unless a valid reason suggested otherwise. France, Belgium and Portugal were hawk-like on the matter. Britain, Greece and Denmark warned that imposing a diplomatic chill against Austria might backfire.

Haider apologized to the Austrian people for once praising the Third Reich's orderly economic program and for describing the SS Waffen troops as "decent men."

An anonymous New York Times news item related that Haider resigned abruptly as leader of the Freedom Party and bowed to international pressure that promised to impose diplomatic and other types of isolation on Austria.

Some political observers thought Haider considered his resignation as a tactical maneuver to keep opponents off balance. The move protected him from criticism of the coalition government while still allowing him to function as governor of the southern province, Carinthia. By resigning, Haider may have had the ultimate goal of becoming Austria's chancellor in mind should the Freedom Party become the dominant political party.

Haider also preferred not to be viewed as a "shadow chancellor" that other ministers looked to for approval. He made it clear, however, that he was "not withdrawing from politics."

Chapter 12

Belgium, Italy, France, Spain, Germany, Congo, Turkey et al European Sites of Resurgent Fervor for "Nationalism"

This chapter describes other European sites where restoration and priority of "nationalist movements" are re-surging in opposition to the borderless immigration policies and its attendant problems. Columnists including Dahlburg, Cohen and Boudreaux and others discuss nationalist movements that are occurring in Belgium, Italy, France, Spain, Germany, Congo, Turkey and elsewhere.

Belgium

Dahlburg discussed "patriotic nationalist" movements in Belgium, Italy, France and Spain. The columnist scribed that a Flemish group on Belgium's "far right," Vlaams Blok, objected to Belgium government's opening a center for "asylum-seeking" immigrants. They proclaimed that "enough is enough, Antwerp was not a garbage can and there were far too many foreigners already." Besides, Antwerp was depressed with unemployment estimated at 12 percent.

The protest for "extreme, patriotic nationalism" in Belgium was viewed by many as a repeat of the "far right's" inclusion in Austria's new coalition government.

"Far right" Belgium nationalists were protesting the borderless, "one-world hegemony"
Where immigrants could inundate each nation and live in "ever present acrimony"
    They want to preserve and practice nationalism,
    Unique culture, loyalty and patriotism,
Not "submit" to "appointed tribunal ideologues who preach "false social harmony"

Dewinter, Flemish leader, predicted that what happened in Austria could happen here. He currently leads the Flemish Blok for separatism and hopes to emulate Haider's Austrian Freedom Party and form a coalition government.

Antwerp was then undergoing "passive ethnic cleansing" as African and East European immigrants "moved in" and the native Flemish "moved out" of neighborhoods as per Dewinter. He suggested that the next "far right" triumph for nationalism might occur in Antwerp.

Italy

In Italy, former Dictator Mussolini's granddaughter Alessandra, Member of Parliament saw the actions as precursors for tougher policies on immigration, crime and security. People were interested in "national rights"—from Italy to Denmark and not in "ideological scare tactics like intolerance of immigrants, separatism or xenophobia."

France

France's Le Pen, too, lauded the success of Haider in Austria despite mutual detest for each other. Le Pen predicted the Freedom Party "would serve the cause of national rights in each country to defend citizens against immigration, crime, insecurity, double digit unemployment, corruption and other problems."

Spain

In Spain, concerns about immigrants were expressed when a "deranged Moroccan immigrant" fatally stabbed a 26-year old Spanish woman.

European Union countries feared an influx of immigrants from a dozen countries extending from Malta to Estonia. Spain feared protests against Moroccan and African immigrants. Italy had its Northern Alliance that wanted a tougher ban on immigrants. Italy said that Albanian immigrants who were racing in cars recently killed three young Italian girls.

Citizens talked of the "return of freedom" and "far right nationalism"
Like Haider's Freedom Party in Austria that exudes "patriotism"
>Outraged Vlaame Blok Party in Belgium,
>Italy's Northern Party not mum,
And Spain's people all fear crime, job-loss and ominous "one-world extremism"

Many nations want to control their borders. The ultimate goal in Belgium is breakup and ultimate independence for the Flanders region according to Dewinter. Certain districts in East Germany were also concerned about immigrants since they have a 30 percent rate of unemployment. Austria and other countries worried about expanding the European Union and its effects on culture and lifestyle. People don't want their "beer and good cooking" taken away by global ideologues.

Germany

Cohen discussed the reemergence of nationalism in Germany that had been close to the surface for a very long time. Dampening "nationalist tendencies and extremist temptations" had been embodied in German politics since World War II

Schaeuble resigned from Germany's Christian Democratic Union, now devoid of leadership, in a time of political "nationalist" crisis sweeping Europe. That is, coupled with the recent rise of Haider's Freedom Party in Austria, "nationalist rights" movements across Europe were emerging from hibernation *"more fearful of globalization than communism."*

Political analyst Moeller viewed the emergence of once hibernating nationalism as troublesome, nevertheless felt the Christian Democratic Party was sufficiently resilient to cope though urgently in need of new blood.

Congo

The 15-member UN Security Council authorized a 5500 security force of "observers" to monitor the implementation of the cease-fire among six nations and three rebel groups in the Congo described an anonymous Associated Press news item. Five hundred observers were included in the expeditionary contingent. Before sending the troops, the UN wanted the former combatants to honor a cease-fire.

Ambassador Holbrooke said the U. S. would not provide troops, only logistical support. The political move may be politically important but not militarily effective because of "few roads and inadequate communication."

Turkey

Turkish generals were reluctant to diminish their nationalist role as Turkey's guardian of internal order despite acceptance into the European Union by its leaders wrote Boudreaux. The Turkish generals, commanders of NATO's second largest military force, have little desire to relinquish their powerful role in government held for 76 years. "It exercises broad constitutional authority to intervene in a lax government when dealing with Kurdish separatism and Islamic fundamentalism."

During the past three years, Turkey's nationalist generals have discarded an Islamic led government, smashed a Kurdish separatist rebellion, convinced Greek Cypriots not to use Russian made missiles against Turkey and gone shopping for tanks and black helicopters.

The EU avidly seeks the generals' submission to civilian control over all internal matters from child labor laws and human rights, structure of its armed forces and its submergence to mini one world European control. (Apparently getting a civilian government to submit to UN dictates is "easier" than "negotiating" military subjugation.)

The generals support EU membership because it meshes with the Founder of the Army and the Republic of Turkey, Kemal Ataturk, and his vision of a secular Europe. In reality, the generals are more desirous of "becoming part of Europe's 'Continental Army' independent of NATO." (In that manner, they maintain more sovereign, nationalist control of its military.)

After EU voted to accept Turkey as a candidate, it required Turkey to "abolish its military dominated National Security Council and subordinate its military staff to a civilian Defense Ministry.

A memo distributed by Turkey's military general staff called EU's requirements as "totally ignorant of Turkish history and a yen to unjustly attack and weaken its armed forces."

Retired Turkish General Bir only promised, "No more coups as change was enough." The Turkish military had taken over direct government rule thrice since 1960. In 1983, their new constitution strengthened their power to "run things behind the scenes."

The military dominated National Security Council, NSC, headed by a four-star general, has its parallel functioning bureaucracy of thousands of government experts who plan and run everything from education to hydroelectric energy to foreign relations. The NSC consists of the Turkish president, four Senior Cabinet Members and five top military commanders who are usually better prepared than civilians. Certain military proposals are deemed as ultimatums.

Although an anti-military sentiment prevails in most European nations, it is weak in Turkey where polls consistently show "75 percent of the people approve the military." Military cadets are taught that "the military is superior to civilians and have a right to intervene when there is instability." More recently, however, the military was criticized because it reacted too slowly in conducting search and rescue operations for victims from a 7.4 earthquake, maltreated civilians in the Kurdish conflict and looked the other way at war profiteers and drug smugglers.

Rumblings are still extant that call for diminished roles of the military and the National Security Council. Some political strategist's thought that the power of the military should be allowed to fade rather than risk open confrontation, then hopefully, democratic rule would evolve in time

Chapter 13

Closing Statement

Diplomatic negotiations for a peace settlement in Kosovo were considered, to some degree, dismal failures that led to Clinton's ordering air strikes on Serbia. Clinton's War of "miscalculation" on Serbia got quickly out of hand because Serbia didn't immediately knuckle under after four days of predominantly U. S. led relentless air strikes. Milosevic, too, erred in resisting, thinking world opinion would be on his side and NATO would fragment from internal bickering on why and how to conduct hostilities.

"Cessation of war" was certainly possible by air strikes alone—but never occupation since enormous "peacekeeper" forces would be necessary to "enforce an uneasy armistice and implement multiethnic integration with its apartheid enclaves" That is, perhaps in the short term at best.

One citizen aptly and tersely expressed sentiments that Clinton economically blackmailed nations to join his war and described the situation as "Clinton's New World Disorder."

Apparently forced integration, peace and living in ethnic harmony was not working. Clashes between Albanian and Serbian forces especially in Mitrovica and elsewhere continued without surcease. The presence of peacekeepers wasn't likely to erase centuries of ethnic hatred that likely still seethed within the innards of Albanians and Serbians. If anything, Clinton's War exacerbated ethnic antagonisms.

There was talk of increasing the numbers of peacekeepers and police officers in Kosovo in order to "quell ethnic disturbances." At the same time, European nations seemed reluctant to deploy more troops, while "globocops" Clinton and Albright were more inclined.

Critics continued to blame Clinton's War as a diversionary move to escape negative repercussions from the alleged Broaddrick rape charge, respite from impeachment and the Monica affair and adverse public impression of China's alleged theft of nuclear secrets.

Patriotism to one's country was attacked as "far right extremism. Scare tactics were widely propagandized in a willing media. The concepts of patriotism, loyalty, separatism and traditional independence, freedom and "just being left alone" were perceived as anathema. Nationalism was condemned and slandered as "virulent, myth-making, tainted ideology, dangerous and twisted thinking" by no less than "America Second," one world zealots who lacked loyalty to no, not one nation. Rather, they waxed loudly and publicly of their allegiance to the " gods of denationalization, desovereignization and international economic-military-political-social control of all nations and their earthling inhabitants."

The easily discernible modus operandi consisted of intentional nefarious polices like "borderless nations, unlimited 'illegal' immigration, fast-tracked, biased, free not fair trade pacts; executive orders, subversion of U. S. military command to foreign commanders, transfer of manufacturing from the U. S. to foreign nations, diversity, multiethnicity, brain washed global education and revisionist history." Incessant omission and/or revision of America's heritage, heroes and tradition and culture became the plan-of-the-day for public education.

Eventually, when the time was deemed propitious, arrogant, "America Second" Clinton took the final, stab in each nation's heart by venturing boldly and commencing his tyrannical "wars of interdependence"—each nation's sovereignty be damned.

At the same time, nationalism was once more emerging throughout Europe because of genuine fears in re borderless nations, unrestrained influx of legal and illegal immigrants, high unemployment, feared loss of jobs and destruction of national culture, liberty, values and individualism. Loyal, patriotic, nationalistic uprisings were occurring across European nations that "dreaded globalism more than communism." The globalists were becoming "itchy in their undergarments and getting antsy."

Attacks on nationalism were widely conducted, promoted and labeled as "excessive, virulent, militant and extreme." Patriotic nationalist individuals who held primary allegiance and loyalty to their own nations were condemned and castigated by arrogant, disdainful, presumptive, zealous, misguided "globalist nation meddlers" as "nationalist ideologues and nationalist myth makers." Everything and everyone who stood in the way of global government would be annihilated. Nothing and no one were going to stand in the way of global government if one-world extremists or zealots had their way.

The globalists, of course, cared not one wit for any individual nation or its sovereign desires. (The situation reminded the writer of Clinton and his appointed "agents of personal destruction" in domestic politics when their lying, adulterous leader was accused of "alleged" infractions. They rose in unison to defend him. Any enemy, real or imagined, had to be attacked and destroyed mercilessly.)

Yet, shamelessly and without conscience, the globalist nation meddlers would "leech" its "fair share" of money, men, materials, management, markets, mercantilism and military from each nation as if "any of the zealots had earned any of these assets or goodies by dint of their own efforts, sacrifice and risk-taking."

Considerable caution was exercised not to offend Muslims and the celebration of Ramadan after "inane, senseless air strikes on Afghanistan and Sudan. Even though the Pope requested Clinton not to bomb on the high holy days of Good Friday, Holy Saturday and Easter, the "one who loathed the military" ordered the merciless bombardment to continue.

Yet, when religious leaders and other nations' representatives made the same request to halt bombings on Muslim's high holy days of Ramadan, he acceded. "Christian" Clinton applied readily his double standard of religious fairness!

Perhaps another contributing reason proclaimed was to "nobly halt ethnic cleansing" of Albanians Muslim rebels who originally provoked sovereign Serbians in Kosovo according to some reporters.

Clinton's military invasions of sovereign nations happened to coincide with several domestic items of unpleasantness burdening Clinton. Among the items of unpleasantness were "Clinton's court-ordered testimony in the Paula Jones case, televised admission of not having sexual relations with that woman (Monica), eve of impeachment hearings and calling off attacks on Iraq after the House voted to impeach him."

Clinton's attack on Serbia was fundamental strategy to implement and enforce the objective of establishing and strengthening the "U. S.—European mini one world order" structure under the propagandist pap cover of world peace, harmony, human rights, ethnic cleansing, national security and so forth. The latter euphemisms were never "paramount" motivations. U. S.—European hegemony was and is of primary import. The globalists never wavered from the sight of this goal.

The modus operandi always focused on several basic stratagems: "destroy and denigrate nationalism and ferociously foster borderless nations" by any means in order to inundate sovereign nations with immigrants designed to foment civil unrest and nibble at nationalism. Such stratagems would serve as excuses for peaceful, military globalist invasion to "restore civil unrest and install nation-splitting pockets of autonomy and independence."

The modus operandi was so vicious in nature that globalists had no hesitation in using the "military as the ultimate, coercive, 'diplomatic' weapon. "They" would never pause to consider any nation's legally established "constitutional government." All constitutions would be sidestepped or ignored by any Machiavellian stratagem whenever the need arose. Only "governments and leaders" approved by the globalist elite would be tolerated. The globalist ideologues were and are devoid of complete dedication, loyalty, patriotism, tradition and honor to any sovereign nation and its traditional culture. Such concepts would be shamelessly shunted aside, feigned and/or glossed over in order to attain global government hegemony.

As America's industrial and manufacturing base and military might continues to be purposely reduced, eliminated, ceded and frittered away to foreign nations, no urgent military need will exist to bomb our economic, superpower might into non-existence. One-sided trade pacts, international financial deals, replacement from a manufacturing to a service industry and globocop involvement in "international crises are incrementally and speedily accomplishing that objective. Imposing "forced peace" is not the real but only an intermediate goal; rather, it is the preferred means of imposing "forced international hegemony or uber alles on all nations" to eventually gather remaining nations into the fold.

Serbia, in fact, was Clinton's "first, large offensive war for interdependence" embarked on by the U. S. and Europe via NATO against a small, fierce, outgunned and out-manned sovereign nation. The attack on Serbia meant that the "alliance" would brook no nonsense from any relatively weak nation that might impede achievement of a "U. S.—Europe mini one world" structure. Submission and obedience were the guideposts or watchwords.

In order to attain its one world objective, the globalists would, however, continue to "negotiate" one-sided trade concessions, loans, largesse, economic sanctions and diplomatic bribes, bluff and bluster when it came to more powerful nations like Russia, China, recalcitrant Turkey and patriotic African countries et al. In essence, "economic diplomacy, not barrel-of- the-gun diplomacy" would be the modus operandi of choice in situations where probable massive military resistance entailing death, injuries and maiming to both military and civilian personnel were likely and expected. "The numerous nations' publics wouldn't tolerate such direct military confrontations." They still cherished freedom and independence to slave-like submission.

Diplomatic negotiations were complete failures in preventing Clinton's War in Serbia. Military intelligence was apparently faulty as evidenced in the erroneous bombing of the Chinese Embassy in Kosovo, the pharmaceutically factory in Sudan and absence of the terrorist leader Osama bin Laden in his hideout in Afghanistan. Faulty intelligence coupled with intermittent bombings designed to locate and destroy the biological, chemical and nuclear weapons of mass destruction in Iraq have also been dismal failures to date.

Seventy-eight days of relentless bombing and decimation of Serbia's infrastructure brought Milosevic to the peace table in belated or "off scheduled" capitulation. Nevertheless, politically astute Milosevic emerged from Clinton's War with his military machine relatively unscathed, still in power and creating civil unrest and havoc in Mitrovica and elsewhere. Some similarities between the Serbian province of Kosovo and Saddam Hussein's plight in Iraq in the aftermath of air strikes ordered by draft dodger Clinton were obvious.

Before Clinton's air strikes were ordered on Kosovo, 200,000 Serbs lived there. That number has been reduced to less than 80,000 with more departing each day. Serbs simply do not trust their security to the "arrangement" existing between Albanians and the peacekeepers. Peaceful coexistence between Albanian Muslims and Serbian Orthodox Christians is "largely political hope but mostly mythical."

General Reinhardt believed that separation of Albanians and Serbians into apartheid enclaves was essential to "prevent the 'pockets of armed enemies' from annihilating each other." Multiethnic integration was "out of the question and realistically simply not possible."

The issue of a new Continental Army was causing consternation among many NATO nations. Many leaders of European nations were tiring of submission to the U. S. and NATO and desired more nationalistic control of their military resources.

Naturally, one world proponent Cohen adamantly opposed the new "Continental Army" because of the specious reason offered that "it siphoned off money and resources needed by NATO." "Submission, submission and more submission of all European nations" to a "mini U. S.—European one-world organization" was the real reason notwithstanding Cohen's lame words of overt opposition.

The second "war of interdependence" supported by the U. S. and NATO occurred in East Timor. The natives in the province rebelled against the Indonesian government, obtained a favorable vote for independence (some say trumped up by UN influence) and requested under pressure, IFOR's invasion of peacekeepers, created a new nation within Indonesia and thereby weakened Indonesia's sovereignty.

IFOR's entry into East Timor was the first "offensive" invasion of sovereign territory in the Far East, the nation of Indonesia. U. S. involvement was essentially "token" in that only military transports were used to deliver men and materials. Other political-diplomatic considerations prevailed.

In any case, the entire episode appeared as an advanced "planned contrivance" since the invasion fleet and forces were already stationed in nearby waters at the time of the vote for independence. Why, because they landed "within days of the vote." Any thinking individual would recognize that logistics for such a multinational sea and air based operation had to be prepared or "in the works" for weeks or months!

With regard to Chechnya, the Russians in effect have informed the West to "mind your own business. Chechnya is an internal matter. Russia heeds your advice in like manner you heeded Russia's counsel on Kosovo."

Albright threatened "diplomatic isolation, delayed loans from the IMF and Export—Import Bank, but was not quite ready to cut off economic aid." She also tried to link the proposed, palliative "token" U. S. anti ballistic missile system with reductions in both nuclear weapon arsenals. Albright would threaten, bluff and bluster but would never sever diplomatic relations because both countries "need each other" for ultimate "mini U. S.—European one world government" purposes.

Critics questioned where the "self-ordained Clinton administration masters of interference in the affairs of sovereign nations" derived their ordination and from whom? The modern "second new-world order" marches on since another nation had been "created by the global meddlers in nation building."

The nationalist situations in Belgium, Italy, France, Spain, Germany and Congo nations and tribes were considered horrendous. They were all in accord that "fervent nationalism" was on the rise and re-emerging. In most countries they believed too many foreigners were entering their countries causing job loss, unemployment, enclaves of acrimonious immigrants, corruption and other social problems. They were displeased with the effects on culture and lifestyle. They all desired tougher laws on immigration, crime and internal security

The situation in Turkey was more unique in that the military is generally revered by the populace, and for all practical purposes, effectively operates the country's government through the National Security Council. Though a member of NATO, the military preferred to become a member of the new "Continental Army" wherein it could maintain maximum control of its military and national sovereignty.

Naturally, the UN preferred that Turkey "surrender" its internal control of the government and peacefully but stupidly relinquishes its governing role to a civilian cabal more receptive and submissive to mini one world U. S.—European hegemony. It remains to be seen if the Turkish military submits and behaves stupidly.

The Turkish situation is in the process of "delicate negotiations" and a final solution is nowhere in sight.

There are additional rumblings and reactions among many nations regarding submission to the one-world dictates of the U. S. and "world governing organizations." Among those heard were Clinton's recent, "legacy" inspired foreign visits that ended in failed attempts to negotiate peace between Irish Catholics and Protestants, India and Pakistan, "Palestine" and Israel and Syria and Israel.

Clinton's policies are reminiscent of an "old world" colonial nation
Uses its "'pol.-econ'—high tech military" might in "forced" negotiation
    Behavior that smacks egomaniacal,
    With odorous effects so tyrannical,
And a bully's disdain for each nation's past, culture, "gov" and organization

Many "nationalist" nations responded to threats of U. S. global dominance
Russia and China pondered a close "partnership" to counter our promi-
nence
    "Only" Britain fought with us in the four-day strike on Iraq,
    Japan planned to form its "intelligence" as a form of "balk,"
And Euro's new "Continental Army" was further "nation loving" evidence

Why any nation would even want to surrender its sovereignty and
nationalism
    To "non-elected," one world ideologues and their unreal, utopian idealism
    Is incomprehensible, stupid, insane,
    A quixotic dream best perceived as a bane,
When the true motives are "political-social power and control through
mercantilism"

Didn't Clinton take the "oath of allegiance to the U. S. Constitution,
not the United Nations" when he was sworn in as president? Doesn't he
remember that this nation fought a Revolutionary War for "independence,
not interdependence" to preserve liberty and freedom from imperious,
oppressive England? Why didn't Clinton respect patriotism, loyalty,
nationalism, devotion, duty, honor and allegiance to the United States,
the country that enabled and afforded him every educational and political
opportunity to "achieve" he ever experienced?

Is his grateful "pay back" or obligation to this great nation merely an
"uber alles" subjugation of the United States, its people and all its blessings
to appointed, not elected, global representatives that bypasses American

voters and cares not one wit for any nation or its inhabitants? His actions are an unforgivable "travesty and sell-out" of this great nation, what it originally fought and sacrificed for and stands for throughout the world. What motivates Clinton to behave like a Machiavellian misanthrope?

The author is reminded of the biblical warning or day of reckoning concerning one's own house (or nation). To paraphrase its gist, "Any disloyal leader that disturbeth one's own nation shall reap the wild wind."

About the Author

Robert R. Morman earned his Masters and Doctorate degrees from USC in psychology. He retired from CSULA in 1992 as a full professor with emeritus status. He served as Chief Yeoman in the USN during WWII and as a Major who retired from the USAFR.

His vocational background comprised four decades plus of experience as a research assistant, pollster, counseling psychologist, college test officer, test constructor, counselor and professor. Among college-university subjects taught were counseling, personality theory, computer introduction, statistics, research, group tests and measurements, individual testing, occupational factors, field/clinic supervision of teachers and counselors, independent study, thesis and dissertation. He also consulted in related fields.

Over 40 technical articles on automation, counseling, statistics, educational research and validating tests were published in various technical journals. Books published include The TAV Selection System, 1968; American Heritage Alternatives to Guaranteed Annual Socialism (co-author R. O. Hankey), 1970; The Clintons' Agenda for Change: Assault on Traditional America, Commonwealth Publications, 1996; Clinton's Planned Betrayal of America "UNAmericanization," 1999, Kabel Publishers, Inc.; and William J. Clinton's Impeachment & Trial, 1999, lst Books Library